Healing
the Soul
of a
Woman

Healing the Soul *of a* Woman

How to Overcome Your Emotional Wounds

JOYCE MEYER

NEW YORK NASHVILLE

FaithWords
Hachette Book Group
1290 Avenue of the Americas, New York, NY 10104
faithwords.com
twitter.com/faithwords

First Edition: September 2018

FaithWords is a division of Hachette Book Group, Inc. The FaithWords name and logo are trademarks of Hachette Book Group, Inc.

The publisher is not responsible for websites (or their content) that are not owned by the publisher.

The Hachette Speakers Bureau provides a wide range of authors for speaking events. To find out more, go to www.hachettespeakersbureau.com or call (866) 376-6591.

Library of Congress Cataloging-in-Publication Data has been applied for.

ISBNs: 978-1-4555-6024-0 (hardcover), 978-1-4555-6026-4 (large type), 978-1-4555-6022-6 (ebook), 978-1-5460-1028-9 (international), 978-1-5460-3525-1 (TBN edition)

Printed in the United States of America

LSC-C

10 9 8 7 6

CONTENTS

Introduction   vii

Chapter 1: The History of Women   1

Chapter 2: Living the Best Life Available   11

Chapter 3: God Wants the Wounded   19

Chapter 4: What Is a Healthy Soul?   29

Chapter 5: Help Me! I Don't Understand Myself   37

Chapter 6: You Are God's Beloved   46

Chapter 7: Hurting People Hurt People   55

Chapter 8: Unload the Guilt and Shame   65

Chapter 9: Finding Your True Self   75

Chapter 10: No Parking at Any Time   84

Chapter 11: You Are Not Damaged Goods   94

Chapter 12: The Wounds of Sin   104

Chapter 13: Learning to Live Inside Out   112

Chapter 14: You've Got What It Takes   122

Chapter 15: Roadblocks to Healing   132

Chapter 16: The Roadblock of Self-Pity   143

Chapter 17: Stand Up for Yourself   151

Chapter 18: Establish Boundaries—Don't Build Walls   159

Chapter 19: Become Your Own Best Ally   168

Chapter 20: Healing the Wounds of Codependency   176

Chapter 21: The Blessings of a Healthy Soul   185

Chapter 22: The Painless Path   194

Chapter 23: The Great Exchange   203

Afterword   211

Appendix I   213

Appendix II: Who You Are in Christ Jesus   225

Endnotes   229

INTRODUCTION

He heals the brokenhearted and binds up their wounds.

—Psalm 147:3 ESV

Can a woman who has been hurt deeply either by circumstances in her life or by a person she loved and trusted be healed? Can her heart and soul be healed? Can she love and trust once again? As a woman who was sexually abused by my father, abandoned by my mother, and cheated on by my first husband, I can say without hesitation, "Yes!" If you are living with a wounded soul and feeling alone, unloved, and misunderstood, I can promise you that you do not have to stay that way.

Beauty for Ashes, which was published in 1994, was the first book I wrote on emotional healing. Since that time I have had a great deal more experience in this area and am more knowledgeable in God's Word, and I want to share those things with you. I have written other books that include some portions of what I will share in this book, but with God's help, this will be an all-inclusive manual from a biblical perspective on the subject of emotional healing.

Countless numbers of people are walking around wounded in their souls from past hurts, and they either don't know they can be healed or simply don't know what to do or how to begin. I will share what I have learned on my journey, and although yours won't be exactly like mine, I hope my story can be an inspiration and a guiding light as you step out onto your path of progress toward wholeness.

Just as our bodies can be sick, our souls can be sick, but God wants to heal us everywhere we hurt, including our soul. The soul is the mind, will, and emotions. It is the inner part of us and a very important part. No matter what we have materially or how good our circumstances are in life, if we have wounded, bruised, and bleeding souls, we will not enjoy life. Whether our hurt is from shame, anger, bitterness, depression, doubt, insecurity, guilt, or fear, it needs to be confronted and dealt with.

I limped through life for years thinking I had the best life I could expect considering my past. I can actually remember thinking as a young adolescent that I would always have a second-rate life because of what my father had done to me. I didn't even attempt to deal with any of the problems that were created from my past simply because I didn't think anything could be done about them. But I was wrong.

It is amazing how wrong our thinking can be, but if we don't know it is wrong then we never rise above it. In this book, I hope to show you that a wonderful, amazing, fulfilling life is available for you. With God's help you can learn to think and behave in ways that will actually set you free to be the amazing woman God created you to be.

Once you know what is available to you, I pray that you will make a decision to go for it! The world offers a variety of remedies for the wounds of the soul, and some of them may be helpful, but Jesus offers us complete healing. He is the healer and restorer of our souls. The psalmist David said God had restored his soul (Psalm 23:3). When something is restored it is made like new once again.

What kind of life did God intend for you as a woman who is

created in His image? It certainly is not one of being minimized, devalued, mistreated, abused, used, and battered. He offers us unconditional love, infinite worth and value, wholeness, righteousness, peace, and joy—and that is just the beginning of His blessings for those who will believe and walk with Him through life!

As you begin the journey of healing for your soul, I ask you to remember that healing takes time. It is also sometimes painful because we have to let old wounds be opened up in order to get the infection that is festering and poisoning our souls out of them. Women who have need of healing for their soul only have two choices. The first is to continue limping along in life, just trying to get through each day, and the second is to say, "I've had enough misery, unhappiness, pretense, guilt, and shame, and I'm ready to do whatever it takes to be made whole!"

Healing
the Soul
of a
Woman

CHAPTER 1

The History of Women

Make the most of yourself, by fanning the tiny sparks of possibility into flames of achievement.

—Golda Meir

First let me say that women are God's idea. Although He created Adam first, He quickly realized that he needed a helper, so He took a rib from Adam's side and created Eve out of it. I like to make the point that Eve was taken from Adam's side, thus indicating she was to walk beside him in life as someone he needed. She was not taken from the bottom of his feet, indicating that he had permission to walk all over her.

If you are familiar with the story of creation (Genesis 1–3), you may know that after God created Adam and Eve, He placed them in a beautiful garden called Eden, and His plan was for them to enjoy life abundantly and fellowship with Him. They had a great deal of freedom to make their own choices and had been endowed with authority to have dominion over the animals and the entire realm they dwelt in. There was, however, one thing God told them not to do, and that was not to eat from the tree of the knowledge of good and evil, of blessing and calamity (Genesis 2:9, 16–17). They could eat from every other tree, including the tree of life. It is clear from this account that God wanted His creation to be filled with life as only He could give it, and in His original intention, He wanted them to know only good and not evil.

Of course, God also knew from the beginning—because He is all-knowing—that Satan, who appeared to Eve as a serpent, would deceive her and that she and Adam would eat of the one tree He had forbidden. That one wrong action opened the door for all the pain and dysfunction that exists on our planet today. You might ask, *Well, if God knew His perfect plan would fail, then why not make it impossible to ruin it?* The answer is very simple: God created man with free will because He wanted to have people to fellowship with who would choose Him, not merely those who had no choice. He wanted people to partner with in life, not puppets that had no choice but to do His bidding.

It is easy to get angry with Adam and Eve and think, *How dumb can you be?* But not one of us would have done any better. Although God created them with free choice, meaning they had the ability to disobey Him, He also from the beginning had a plan for the complete restoration and wholeness of men and women. That plan, simply stated, is *Jesus*.

God loves us so much that He planned from the beginning of time to let His only Son pay for our sins and bring us full salvation. Salvation means life, but the life that God offers us is not merely an ability to breathe and walk around—He offers us "life" as only God knows it. We can be filled with the life of God. That life is so powerful that no matter what has happened to us in the past that has damaged our souls, we can be healed and totally restored. All death is swallowed up in life, and darkness is swallowed up in light. Jesus is both Life and Light. That's why John 1:4 says, "In Him was Life, and the Life was the Light of men."

I can assure you that God is never without a plan. And no

matter what has happened to you, God has a plan for you, and it is a good plan.

After Satan successfully deceived Eve, tempting her to be disobedient, God made a statement to him that leads us to understand why women, by and large throughout history, have been so marginalized, disrespected, and devalued. Genesis 3:14–15 says:

> And the Lord God said to the serpent, Because you have done this, you are cursed above all [domestic] animals and above everything [wild] living thing of the field; upon your belly you shall go, and you shall eat dust [and what it contains] all the days of your life.
>
> And I will put enmity between you and the woman, and between your offspring and her Offspring; He will bruise *and* tread your head underfoot, and you will lie in wait *and* bruise His heel.

Please notice that the "Offspring" of Eve is capitalized in this verse, but the offspring of the serpent is not. That is because the offspring of Eve is Jesus Christ. She is the mother of all living beings and is directly in the ancestral line of Jesus. God was letting Satan know that Eve's Offspring would bruise his head, or take his authority away from him and defeat him. Satan would, for a time, bruise the heel of God's children, referring to how he attacks us in our daily walk.

This same type of attack was perpetrated against Jesus during His time on earth, but the end of the story is that Jesus died in our place, took our pain and sorrow, suffered beyond anything we can imagine, and paid for our sins. But thankfully that isn't the end of the story. If it were, it would have given Satan the victory he always hoped to have. He had indeed bruised the heel of our

Savior. But Jesus was in the grave three days, during which time He took possession of "the keys of death and Hades (the realm of the dead)" (Revelation 1:18), and then He rose from the dead, and He is alive forevermore! Through the Offspring of Eve (Jesus), God bruised Satan's head (authority).

Satan has been stripped of the authority that Adam and Eve gave to him through their disobedience, but if we don't know that he is defeated, we will continue to let his wicked and evil plan rule in our lives. Satan is defeated, and a life filled with healing and abundance is available to you! All you need to do in order to receive it is to receive Jesus as your Savior by faith and believe that the promises in God's Word are for you. As you do, you will step out into a lifetime journey with Jesus, who will guide you along your path.

No matter how deep a pit you may feel you are in, God's arm is not too short to reach in and lift you out. He will set you on high places and give you peace that passes all understanding and joy that you cannot describe. God will meet you where you are and help you get to where you need to be.

Satanic Attack on Women

The cruel and unjust treatment of women down through the ages can only be attributed to a demonic attack. I will give you a few statistics that I am aware of just to make my point. (See appendix I for more statistics.)

VOTING RIGHTS:

- Ratified on August 18, 1920, the Nineteenth Amendment to the US Constitution granted American women the right to vote—a right known as women's suffrage. At the time the

US was founded, its female citizens did not share all of the same rights as men, including the right to vote.[1]

EQUAL PAY AND PROPERTY RIGHTS:

- On average, women employed full-time in the United States lose a combined total of more than $840 billion every year due to the wage gap.[2]

EDUCATION:

- Globally, 65 million girls are not in school.[3]
- Two-thirds of the 774 million illiterate people in the world are female.[4]
- If all women had a primary education, there would be 15 percent fewer child deaths. If all women had a secondary education, child deaths would be cut in half, saving 3 million lives. Mothers' education improves child nutrition. If all women had a primary education, 1.7 million children would be saved from stunted growth due to malnutrition.[5]

GENDERCIDE:

- Demographers estimate that 126 million women are missing due to gendercide (the murder of someone based on their sex, also called femicide). That is as many deaths as those caused by World Wars I and II and AIDS combined. Every year, we lose 2 million baby girls to sex-selective abortion and infanticide. That's four girls per minute. In China alone, 62 million women are missing. That amounts to 9.5 percent of its female population.[6]

- Gendercide affects women of all ages but bears down especially hard on the youngest. In the last twenty years, sex-selective abortion has displaced infanticide as the primary method for eliminating baby girls.[7]

VIOLENCE AND ABUSE AGAINST WOMEN:

- It is estimated that 35 percent of women worldwide have experienced either physical or sexual violence by an intimate partner or sexual violence by a nonpartner at some point in their lives. However, some national studies show that up to 70 percent of women have experienced physical or sexual violence from an intimate partner in their lifetime.[8]
- Adult women account for almost half of all human trafficking victims detected globally. Women and girls together account for about 70 percent, with girls representing two out of every three child-trafficking victims.[9]

HUMAN TRAFFICKING:

- Women and girls make up 98 percent of victims of trafficking for sexual exploitation.[10]
- The average age a teen enters the sex trade in the US is twelve to fourteen years old. Many victims are runaway girls who were sexually abused as children.[11]
- According to the US State Department, human trafficking is one of the greatest human rights challenges of this century, both in the US and around the world.[12]

Thankfully, women have made some progress, especially in the Western world, but women are still abused even there. And in many other parts of the world a lot of the things I described on the previous pages are still taking place daily. The battle for the freedom and restoration of women is ongoing, but I am glad I know that healing can occur through faith in God, and I am glad that our ministry is part of helping to bring this freedom to women worldwide.

Because of a long history of being devalued and dishonored, many women today, even in places where a lot of progress has been made, still don't see their true worth and value. They doubt their abilities, and in many instances won't even try to do great things with their life simply because of a wrong mind-set that is ingrained in them. "I'm just a woman" is a statement that I dislike hearing. That very statement is telling in itself.

I remember that when God called me to the ministry, I began experiencing a lot of rejection, for no reason other than I was a woman, and women didn't teach God's Word. I heard things like, "Women can teach Sunday school, but they are not permitted to teach in the main church service." This made no sense, because if it was improper for them to teach, then it would be just as improper to teach Sunday school as it would be to teach in the main church service, or to be a pastor or an evangelist, or to hold any other type of office in the church world.

I was judged, criticized, asked to leave my church, and ostracized by family and friends to the point where I went to God in prayer and reminded Him that I was a woman, and therefore I could not do the things I felt in my heart I was to do. I distinctly remember hearing God whisper to my heart, "Joyce, I know you are a woman!" He wanted me to continue doing what He was leading me to do no matter how much opposition I got. Thankfully, over the years many people's minds have changed, but not all of them. Hopefully, we will still see the day when women are permitted to take their rightful place in all of society and be respected, valued, and appreciated.

Some women who have decided to fight for their rights have become rebellious and have attitudes that are not healthy for them or the world we live in. It is understandable why the women's liberation movement was started. Women were so tired of being oppressed that they finally decided to blast their way out of bondage. However, in the process many women are now in danger of having an attitude that is excessive and not in agreement with God's will.

God did clearly give Adam (men) authority over Eve (women), but not to rule her. It was for her protection. Women have an innate desire to be taken care of, to be treasured, and to feel safe, and men should provide that. Since that did not occur, at least not in many cases, women have begun to take over and do what in many instances men should be doing. Had things worked properly from the beginning of time, this imbalance would not exist, but they didn't work properly, and, sadly, the beautiful relationship between men and women that God intended has been lost. We dare not look to the world to teach us in these areas, but we can look to God's Word; by obeying godly principles in Scripture, we can experience a healthy balance that will be a blessing to everyone.

I am a woman in ministry, the head of an international ministry, and yet I am also a woman who respects her husband's authority. Dave and I love and respect and submit to one another as unto the Lord. I have had a lot to learn because of being abused by a variety of male authority figures on hundreds of occasions, and it didn't come easily, but God has helped me see His original plan for the respectful, peaceful coexistence of men and women, and I pray I might always model that for those I have the privilege of teaching.

Thankfully, our history does not have to be our destiny. I often say, "I didn't have a good start in life, but I am determined to have a good finish!" If you have a wounded soul that is in need of healing, I pray that you will make that same decision and declaration.

> *I didn't have a good start in life, but I am determined to have a good finish!*

Attitude

Many books have been written about the danger of a bad attitude and the power of a good one. This section is not intended to be a deep and thorough study of the subject, but I do want to mention it. Like most people who have wounded souls, I had a very bad attitude. In my head it sounded something like this: *No man is ever going to push me around again! Nobody is going to tell me what to do from now on. I will take care of myself, so I never need to ask anyone for anything. You cannot trust men because they are only interested in using you for their own selfish interests. I will never again be put in a position for anyone to be able to hurt me.*

These thoughts and many others like them played over and over in my mind for years and years. My attitude was hardened and my mind was set. If this describes you in any way at all, I suggest that after inviting Jesus into your heart, you invite Him into your attitude. I won't tell you that you will never get hurt again if you open your heart and let people into your life, but I can promise you that if you do get hurt, Jesus, your Healer, will be with you to help you once again. If we spend our lives trying to protect ourselves from ever being hurt, we will also spend our lives lonely.

The apostle Paul wrote to the Philippians, instructing them to let the same humble attitude be in them that was in Christ Jesus (Philippians 2:5–8). The thought of humbling ourselves to anyone else is frightening because we see it as weakness and assume that if we show any weakness, we will be taken advantage of. But actually, meekness and humility are strength under control, not weakness. When Dave and I have a disagreement about a decision that needs to be made, I don't enjoy it if I don't get my way, and I will admit that I still need a lot of help from God in order to give in with a good attitude. But I also know if I do what God asks just because it is the right thing to do, then He will always take care of me, and He will do the same thing for you.

You always win when God fights on your side.

Part of the restoration that God offers us is to have a healthy attitude, one that knows when to take a stand against things that are wrong and when to give in and do what someone else is asking us to do to. I am so grateful to God that I no longer have to feel like I am fighting the world, trying to get what is rightfully mine, and I am thrilled to have this opportunity to teach you that you don't have to live that way. God wants to fight your battles, and believe me when I say that when God fights on your side, you always win!

CHAPTER 2

Living the Best Life Available

In Him was Life, and the Life was the Light of men.

—John 1:4

"Ah, the good life!" When we hear that phrase we may think of lying on a beach day after day, or being able to buy the new automobile we have admired, or owning a yacht and fishing off the deck. But that kind of life has proven *not* to be the best because many people who do have that kind of life will admit that they are unhappy, lonely, and miserable. I heard that Jay Gould, an American millionaire, had plenty of money, but when he was dying, he said, "I suppose I am the most miserable man on earth."

There is nothing wrong with having those things, but they are not life; they are things. God offers us true life through Jesus Christ—a real life, the best life that anyone can possibly live. He offers us a life of being made right with God, and one of peace and joy (Romans 14:17). Jesus said that He came so that we might have abundant life, "to the full, till it overflows" (John 10:10).

The best kind of life is only found in God because He is life, and the life that we call ours is a gift from Him. He is the giver of life!

Do You Need an Upgrade?

Many different types of technology are available to us today, two of them being computers and cell phones. The companies who sell these devices are regularly offering upgrades, and most of us rush to get them. We waste no time, we spend money, wait in lines, whatever it takes to get the newest upgrade. We want the best equipment that is available.

If we are that aggressive about technology, why wouldn't we want the best life available and be equally aggressive in making sure we have it? Just as you have to learn how to work the new upgrade you get, we have to learn how to work with God and His plan for our lives.

I've had a relationship of some sort with God since I was nine years old. During that time I've had many upgrades. I've continued to learn things and understand more fully what is available to me through my relationship with Him. So, you may know nothing at all, or perhaps you are educated in Scripture, but I think all of us still fall short of fully living the life God has made available through Christ, and that includes me. That is why we need to continue growing and learning. It is a process that continues throughout our lives, and I might add, it is one that I believe is very exciting. Why not make a commitment right now to spend the rest of your life learning how to enjoy the best life God has available to you through Jesus Christ? Ephesians 2:10 talks about that life when it says:

> For we are God's [own] handiwork (His workmanship), recreated in Christ Jesus, [born anew] that we may do those good works which God predestined (planned beforehand) for us [taking paths which He prepared ahead

of time], that we should walk in them [living the good life which He prearranged and made ready for us to live].

Sometimes we have a tendency when reading a book to skim over the Scriptures that an author uses, so I want to ask you to stop reading for a moment and go back and slowly read the Scripture I just quoted and really think about what it is saying to you.

Let me give you my paraphrase: *God created us; we are His workmanship. Because of sin we lived broken lives, but through the salvation offered in Jesus we are born again, or made new once again. We get to start over and learn how to do things right. God has always had a good plan for His people and He always will. It is available to anyone who will choose it and learn how to walk in it.*

I received a major upgrade in 1976. You might even say it was a complete system overhaul, and it came as a result of crying out to God for change because I was sick and tired of being so miserable. He answered my cry by giving me a genuine desire to study His Word and start learning what was available to me. Before this time, I had been a Christian for many years, attending church and trying to be good. Like many people, I had a mistaken idea about what it meant to be a Christian. We often reduce it to church attendance, perhaps putting a little money in the offering basket, saying a prayer when we are desperate, maybe reading a little Scripture occasionally, and trying to be good. But that kind of life is never fulfilling; all it does is leave us frustrated. We become confused because we think we are doing what we should be doing, but our lives are still quite miserable.

But as I studied God's Word and applied what I was learning, amazing changes began to happen in me—in my soul. I will admit that it was not always quick or easy, and it was often painful, especially emotionally. For example, I had to admit my faults and stop blaming all of my problems on my past and other people, and that was hard! Because when a person has lived in denial for a long time, it is not always easy to face truth. It is similar to getting a new upgrade on your phone. You wanted it, but once you got it, maybe you didn't bother to learn all of the new features because the old way is just easier. At least that is what I do.

I cannot even imagine all I could do with my computer and phone if I took the time to actually learn all of the features and practice them until I was good at using them. Once in a while, my son will need to help me with something that has gotten messed up on my computer, and when he sees some of the antiquated methods I am still using even though I have new equipment, he simply says, "You have no idea how much easier this would be if you learned the new way."

A New Way of Living

Jesus said He is the Way (John 14:6). In the very early days of Christianity, it was often called "the Way." God's plan includes a way to live that will lead us to everything good He offers. This plan begins with receiving Jesus as our Savior. One may faithfully attend church and still not be a Christian. Christianity is not merely belonging to a church and trying to be a good person, but it is about Jesus and what He has done for us. He offers us Himself as the sacrifice and payment for our sins and guilt, and when we receive Him, He actually comes by His Spirit to live, dwell, and make His home in us. Once you are born again (repent of sin and receive Jesus as Savior), you no longer need to be led by rules and regulations, expecting to get some reward from God if you keep them

> *Christianity is not merely belonging to a church and trying to be a good person.*

all, but you can be led and prompted by the Holy Spirit, who will guide you into the full plan of God for your life. It truly is a whole new way of living.

The New Testament book of Hebrews talks about the new and living way that Jesus had opened up through His death and resurrection (Hebrews 10:20). There are things to be learned about the new way of living that will seem uncomfortable or perhaps a bit unusual, because they are different from anything you have learned previously. One of those things is God's instruction to forgive our enemies, those who abuse and misuse us, and to actually love and bless them. Wow! That was a hard one for me. Forgive my father, who had stolen my childhood through using me as a means to vent his own lust? Forgive my mother? She knew what my father was doing to me, and instead of rescuing me, she pretended she knew nothing and treated me as if I were doing something wrong. Forgiving them seemed totally unreasonable to me, and it took a long time for me to become willing to do it, and even then it was painful.

This is only one of many things that God has shown me about this new way of living, and that is why I say it is a lifetime journey. I am still learning. But I want to be very clear that each path the Holy Spirit has led me down on this new way has always ended up bringing me to a better place than where I was previously. God will never ask us to do anything difficult unless it will lead us to a better life. If you can begin your journey believing that, it may well make your journey shorter than mine was.

Like our computer programs, learning the new way can be challenging, and it may be tempting to revert to old ways, but if we persist in the new way, it will lead us to greater fruitfulness and ease. Throughout this book I will share many of the new ways that God is offering you, and I sincerely pray that you take advantage of each one of them.

Loving God's Word

I love my Bible. It is so much more than a mere book; it is filled with life. It teaches us the new way of living, and in the process we begin to experience healing for our wounded souls and hope for the future. Solomon wrote about the healing found in following God's instruction when he said:

> My son, attend to my words; consent *and* submit to my sayings. Let them not depart from your sight; keep them in the center of your heart. For they are life to those who find them, healing *and* health to all their flesh (Proverbs 4:20–22).

God's words are life to us and bring healing to every area of our life, including our inner life (soul). Our entire being is healed through the life-giving power of God's Word. His Word will do amazing things in our life if we will believe it. God's Word renews our mind and teaches us an entirely new way to think about God, life, ourselves, and other people.

Like many people, I once thought I knew a lot, but most of what I had learned prior to studying God's Word was wrong. I knew what the world had taught me, and I knew what I felt like, but I knew nothing about the new way of living that God wanted to teach me. God's Word is a light for your path (Psalm 119:105). Study it and do what it says to do, and you will be healed and made whole.

God's Word is medicine for our wounded souls. You might ask,

"How can studying a book become medicine for the emotional wounds from my past?" Let me explain it by using an example. If you go to the pharmacy and get a prescription filled, you go home with pills and begin taking them. Inside the pills there is medicine that promises to heal your infection, stop your pain, or heal whatever is hurting you. You take the medicine diligently, and if you are still having problems, you get it refilled and do it again. God's Word is also full of life-giving, healing power. It may look like a book with words on pages, but when it is taken into your heart diligently and you believe it, it truly does have amazing healing power.

God's Word is filled with promises for those who act on what He says to do, and these promises are for everyone who believes and puts their trust in Him.

> God's Word is medicine for your wounded soul.

If Bible study sounds daunting to you, or if perhaps you think that you could never understand the Bible, then I suggest that you join a group of godly people who are on the same path as you are and study together. Find one that has a good reputation, with a leader who is experienced in the areas you need help in.

Another way you might receive help is through group therapy, which has helped many people, and it gives you an opportunity to be with people who can truly have empathy for what you have gone through. If you are unable to locate such a group, I can assure you that the Holy Spirit will lead you Himself, as an individual, just as He did me. I was made whole through reading various Bible-based books on the areas I needed help in, as well as Bible study, sitting under good biblical teaching in my church, and prayer and fellowship with God.

If you need healing for your soul and you don't know where to go to get help, I suggest that you ask God to lead you down the healing path He has planned for you. He will lead you just as He did me, and millions of others. As you follow His guidance, you will experience the same healing and wholeness that we have.

The goal of every hurting person is to be healed, and a variety of paths can be taken. It is very important that you choose a path that is based on God's Word and His promises; otherwise, you could end up becoming more and more frustrated as you put time, effort, and perhaps a lot of money into something that never produces any good results. I know people who paid hundreds of thousands of dollars on treatment programs that promised healing and deliverance, and yet they never got any better until they let Jesus into their life and began depending on Him and following His ways.

The important thing is that you make a decision to get the help you need if you are someone who is living with wounds and bruises in your soul from past or current situations that need to be healed. An amazing life is waiting for you, one of peace and joy, filled with hope and enthusiasm. It is a life you don't want to miss!

CHAPTER 3

God Wants the Wounded

The unwounded life bears no resemblance to the Rabbi.
—Brennan Manning

Our true problem lies not in being wounded but in whether or not we are willing to be healed. God actually uses our wounds to give us wisdom and to equip us to bring light into the darkness of other wounded souls. Brennan Manning said, "In a futile attempt to erase our past, we deprive the community of our healing gift. If we conceal our wounds out of fear and shame, our inner darkness can neither be illuminated nor become a light for others."[13]

> *The problem lies not in being wounded but in whether or not we are willing to be healed.*

God wants soldiers in His army who have allowed Him to heal their wounded souls. No matter who has rejected you in the past, I can assure you that Jesus will not reject you. If you have ever felt that God could never use you because of your past, consider what Paul wrote to the church in Corinth:

> For [simply] consider your own call, brethren; not many [of you were considered to be] wise according to human estimates *and* standards, not many influential *and* powerful, not many of high *and* noble birth (1 Corinthians 1:26).

Perhaps you lack the education that would qualify you for certain positions, but your normal education doesn't matter that much to God. He can use you with it or without it. Perhaps you don't know any influential or powerful people, but that doesn't matter because God can give you favor. "For the Lord sees not as man sees; for man looks on the outward appearance, but the Lord looks on the heart" (1 Samuel 16:7). And 1 Corinthians 1:27–28 says:

> [No] for God selected (deliberately chose) what in the world is foolish to put the wise to shame, and what the world calls weak to put the strong to shame.
>
> And God also selected (deliberately chose) what in the world is lowborn *and* insignificant and branded *and* treated with contempt, even the things that are nothing, that He might depose *and* bring to nothing the things that are.

God deliberately chooses those who have been wounded to work in His Kingdom army. He works through their wounds and weaknesses, and people see His power. When people in the world think they are strong and have all the qualifications they need, but they are not leaning and relying on God, He often has to pass them over and instead choose someone who is less qualified from a worldly perspective but is entirely dependent upon Him in all areas of their life. As you put your trust in God, the day may come when even the people who hurt you will witness the mighty things that God has done in your life and through you as His instrument.

Being experienced is a benefit, but getting the experience is painful. Instead of thinking about how much you have gone through in life that has been painful, why not think about all the experience that you now have, and all the opportunities that are before you as God's daughter? Remember, with God there are no rejects. That's why Jesus said:

> He who believes in Him [who clings to, trusts in, relies on Him] is not judged [he who trusts in Him never comes up for judgment; for him there is no rejection, no condemnation—he incurs no damnation] ... (John 3:18).

If you were to apply for a job, one question that is guaranteed to be on your application is "How much experience do you have?" The employer will probably be interested in your level of education, but if two people apply who are equally educated and one has experience in the area they are applying to work in and the other one doesn't, the more experienced worker will almost certainly get the job.

Experience gives us something that nothing else can. We learn by God's Word and by life's experience (Proverbs 3:13). It is easy to talk about a thing, but only experience makes what we say worth listening to. The world is filled with people who judge what they know nothing about and attempt to educate people regarding what they have never experienced.

> It's easy to talk, but only experience makes what we say worth listening to.

I remember a psychologist who told me that she would sit with her patients and ramble on and on while being aware that she really wasn't helping them, and sometimes even feeling that she didn't know what she was talking about. After reading my original book on inner healing, *Beauty for Ashes*, and my first book on the mind, *The Battlefield of the Mind*, she said that she listened to people who came to her, letting them talk about their pain, and when it came time to offer advice she prescribed those two books for them. She was educated in psychology, but I had experience; therefore, her education and my experience worked together to help her patients.

I am not suggesting that every psychologist and psychiatrist needs to have experienced everything their patients have gone through, but I do think their education is enhanced greatly if they have had to apply the principles they are teaching to their own lives.

We are prone to despising the painful things we have gone through in life, but God can use them to help others if we will let Him. I don't for one second believe that God arranged for my abuse so He could give me some experience, but I do believe that He has used my experience to help other people, and He will do the same thing with your experience in life.

God uses everyone who is willing to be used by Him, but there are a few positions in Kingdom work that only the experienced can fill. If someone is hurting, it is very frustrating and useless to try to talk to someone about it if they can plainly see that the person has no practical idea what they are going through. When we are hurting, we need empathy, and the best person to give us that is someone who has been where we are.

What Qualifies Jesus to Help Us?

Your initial reaction to that question might be, "Well, Joyce, He is the Son of God. Doesn't that qualify Him?" But the Bible says that Jesus chose to experience our pain.

Although He was a Son, He learned [active, special] obedience through what He suffered and, [His completed experience] making Him perfectly [equipped], He became the Author *and* Source of eternal salvation to all those who give heed *and* obey Him (Hebrews 5:8–9).

These two Scripture verses speak volumes to me not only about Jesus but also about my own life. Jesus needed experience in order to be our High Priest so He could truly say that He understood our pain. My experience with Jesus' healing power qualifies me to boldly tell others that Jesus will heal their wounded souls just as He has mine.

Jesus suffered. He gained experience. And it equipped Him for what His Father wanted Him to do. Paul wrote that we have a High Priest who is able "to understand and sympathize and have a shared feeling with our weaknesses," because He has gone through the things we go through now (Hebrews 4:15). I am amazed each time I read and contemplate these Scriptures, and they give me hope that what I have been through will be used to help other people.

God is good and therefore He can take what Satan intended for harm and work it out for our good and the good of others who need help. We are soldiers in God's mighty army, but instead of putting His soldiers who are wounded in a hospital, He actually promotes them into positions of greater power and influence.

When Moses reached a point in his life where he needed help, God told him to find wise, understanding, experienced, and respected men and promote them (Deuteronomy 1:13). I urge you at this moment to offer your experience to God for His use if you have never done that. I vividly recall saying to God, "I am a broken mess, but I'm Yours if You can use me," and He did. Anything we give to God will never be wasted. He takes the broken pieces of our lives and makes beautiful things. He gives us

> *God's story never ends with ashes.*

beauty for ashes. Elisabeth Elliot said, "Of one thing I am perfectly sure, God's story never ends with ashes."[14]

That statement touches me deeply and gives me hope. We may begin with ashes, but when we give them to Jesus, He makes something beautiful. Don't let your pain be wasted by being bitter and resentful throughout life because you feel that you have been unjustly treated. Instead, make your experiences a valuable tool for helping others.

God gave this word to Isaiah to give to the people who were in fear because of the painful things they were going through:

> Behold, I will make you to be a new, sharp, threshing instrument which has teeth; you shall thresh the mountains and beat them small, and shall make the hills like chaff.
>
> You shall winnow them, and the wind shall carry them away, and the tempest *or* whirlwind shall scatter them. And you shall rejoice in the Lord, you shall glory in the Holy One of Israel.
>
> The poor and needy are seeking water when there is none; their tongues are parched with thirst. I the Lord will answer them; I, the God of Israel, will not forsake them (Isaiah 41:15–17).

If you read this carefully, you will see that God promises to take you and turn you into a valuable tool that can be used to help those who are seeking help. I love the thought of being a new, sharp, threshing instrument that can be used to beat the mountains into pieces so tiny that the wind can blow them away. Multitudes of people have mountains looming in front of them that they feel they can never overcome, but you can use your experience to help them.

Sanctified Experiences

The psalmist David spoke about sanctified experiences that he had (Psalm 119:7). The word *sanctified* means set apart for God's use, consecrated, or declared holy. The painful and unjust things that happen to us in life don't come from God, but He can sanctify them for His own use. I love this thought. Satan is our true enemy, and in reality, he is behind all of our pain and suffering, but by letting God sanctify those pains and use them to help others, we have found the secret of overcoming evil with good (Romans 12:21).

If you don't like what the devil has done in your life or the destruction he has caused, then don't play into his hands by being resentful, angry, and filled with self-pity. Instead, let God sanctify your pain, and you will see the fulfillment of the Scripture that says the enemy may come against you one way, but he will flee before you seven ways (Deuteronomy 28:7). You no longer have to spend your life running from the pain of your past; you can put the devil (your true enemy) on the run.

Many different types of things happen to women that wound their souls, but none of them need to be wasted. Here is a short list of some of the things that wound us:

- Abuse of any kind
- Being bullied

- Being battered by a violent spouse
- An unfaithful husband
- Death of a child or a spouse
- Long-term illness
- Divorce
- Stress of being a caregiver
- Rejection
- Being marginalized (by a parent, spouse, friend, or employer)
- Betrayal of a friend
- Being the subject of gossip or lies
- A child who is ill or in pain
- A loved one who is following a destructive path in life
- Prejudice
- Being the victim of a crime
- Inability to have children
- Inability to meet the expectations of others
- Struggles with weight, acne or some other physical imperfection
- Feeling like you are never enough—never smart enough, pretty enough, good enough

Any of these violations can be redeemed by God and used for His glory. There is nothing that has hurt you that can scar you for life. There is nothing that you cannot recover from, and nothing that God cannot heal.

> *There is nothing that God cannot heal.*

Marked for Life

Abuse can be sexual, emotional, mental, or physical. Abuse of any kind is damaging, but it is said that sexual violation is the most destructive to a woman's soul. Physical, emotional, or sexual child abuse is said to mark women's brains in certain patterns. Hearing that could leave a person feeling they would be marked in a negative way for the rest of their life, but I have good news: We are marked and branded and sealed by the Holy Spirit, and we are preserved for God's special use no matter what we have gone through.

> In Him you also who have heard the Word of Truth, the glad tidings (Gospel) of your salvation, and have believed in *and* adhered to *and* relied on Him, were stamped with the seal of the long-promised Holy Spirit.
>
> That [Spirit] is the guarantee of our inheritance [the firstfruits, the pledge and foretaste, the down payment on our heritage], in anticipation of its full redemption and our acquiring [complete] possession of it—to the praise of His glory (Ephesians 1:13–14).

The seal of the Holy Spirit guarantees that we will be fully redeemed and acquire complete possession of our inheritance in Christ. No matter how wounded we are when we begin our journey toward wholeness, God has guaranteed our success as long as we don't give up. He gathers up the fragments of our broken lives and makes sure that nothing is wasted.

In order to better understand the full meaning of what the seal of the Holy Spirit represents, let me give you a little history from the time Paul wrote the letter to the Ephesians. Ephesus was a town with many logging businesses. Workers went into the forests upstream from the river that ran through the town and cut down logs that would be marked or branded with the seal of the logging company they worked for. These logs were floated downstream and held in docks in Ephesus until their owners needed them for a project. Because they were marked with a seal representing ownership, they were protected from theft.

We have been bought with a price and that price is the blood of Jesus; we have been sealed with the Holy Spirit to protect us while we are waiting for our full redemption. The devil comes only to steal, kill and destroy, but Jesus came that we might have and enjoy our lives (John 10:10).

You have been sealed and marked by God.

You have been sealed and marked by God. You are His. You are safe.

One of the things that women want is to feel safe, and I want you to know that you are safe with God.

You are set apart (sanctified) for God's use, and that includes any and everything that you have gone through that was painful or damaging. I urge you to release all of your past pain and wounds to the Holy Spirit and ask Him to begin His restoration project in your life. Don't waste your pain—let God work it out for your good.

CHAPTER 4

What Is a Healthy Soul?

Truly my soul finds rest in God; my salvation comes from him.

—Psalm 62:1 NIV

The soul of a woman is rather a mystical place because it cannot be seen and is rarely understood, even by the woman herself. Still, it holds a place of importance in our overall makeup. We know what our body is because all we have to do is look in the mirror and see it. We may not like what we see, but at least we know what it is. We are spiritual beings who have a soul and live in a body. Your inner self is composed of your spirit and soul, and your outer self is your body.

The spirit of a woman is where the Holy Spirit comes to live when she is born again. When she receives Jesus as her Savior, her spirit becomes the dwelling place of God, and since God cannot be anywhere that is not completely holy, the human spirit is sanctified, or made holy, at that point. We actually receive everything we need to live amazingly wonderful lives at that point, but since we lack knowledge, it takes time and diligent study of God's Word in order for us to understand it. And even after we know what we have, we still need to make decisions to act accordingly. Knowing is step 1, but it needs to be followed by step 2, which is doing what we now know.

For example, Jesus is the Prince of Peace, so since He is living in the woman of God, she does indeed have peace at her disposal, yet she may still worry, be anxious, and display emotions that are erratic. To be erratic is to be unstable, unpredictable, inconsistent, changeable, or fitful. Once she decides she no longer wants to live and behave that way, being manipulated by her circumstances, she will begin the process of retraining the emotional part of her soul to come under the guidance of the Holy Spirit that is within her. She will need to rely on God to give her the strength to obey Him, and if she has been fiercely independent, this may take some time and could include several failed attempts at remaining peaceful in the storms of life before she begins to see changes.

In order not to become discouraged, it is important to remember that God has promised that He will complete the good work He has begun in us (Philippians 1:6). Our part is to keep pressing toward the goal and to never give up. Eventually, little by little, our soul will find its rest in God.

We know what it is like to sit or lie down and rest our bodies, but we may not know what it is like to rest internally, in the realm of the soul. When we are at complete rest in mind, will, and emotion, then and only then will we be free from the tyranny of circumstances and people that upset us. We cannot control all of the circumstances of life, or the people in our lives, but God has given us the fruit of self-control, and with His help we can learn to control our response to what takes place around us. This is true freedom.

A healthy soul is at rest; it is not emotionally distraught. It doesn't worry or become anxious, fret, and fear. It is not burdened with guilt or shame. It has found its home in God and trusts Him to take care of all that concerns it. Admittedly, in our world today there is an abundance of things to be concerned about. If you are a single mother trying to raise children on your own or you have a special needs child or you are continually under financial pressure, facing illness, or the caretaker for elderly parents, it may sound ludicrous to say, "You can have rest in your soul." If you feel that way, I totally understand how you feel. But nothing is impossible with God, and you can have a supernatural rest that only He can give.

Responsibility

We all have lots of responsibility and we cannot ignore it. Women take care of a lot of things even if they have good husbands, but for a single parent that responsibility is magnified. A woman may say she is going to bed and end up doing ten minor chores while on her way, but a man says he is going to bed and he does. One of my daughters has four teenagers. I had three teenagers and a baby thirty-seven years ago when I was just beginning the ministry, so I know how challenging it can be. But life was not quite as complicated as it is today.

I watch my daughter go from thing to thing to thing, and it seems like it is an everyday occurrence. Her husband just went on a fishing trip, and she thought she was going to get a few days in her home that were a bit calmer. She planned on some time for herself, and she was excited. The very first day she thought she was finally alone, the school called; one of her daughters was sick and needed to be picked up. Then her son who is in college came home from school in the afternoon and wanted to bring his girlfriend over. Her alone time didn't happen. Life happened.

We have responsibilities. God invites us to cast our care (1 Peter 5:7), not to ignore our responsibilities. It is amazing how

much easier things are if we do them without the stress we normally carry in our souls. I believe our energy actually increases
greatly when we are at rest in our
souls and have internal peace. I
don't know any other way to get rid
of the stress we experience today
other than learning to trust God at all times, in all things.

> *God invites us to cast our care,
> not to ignore our responsibilities.*

Jesus said that if we would come to Him, then He would give
us rest for our souls.

> Come to Me, all you who labor and are heavy-laden *and*
> overburdened, and I will cause you to rest. [I will ease
> and relieve and refresh your souls] (Matthew 11:28).

If we read the next verse, we see that enjoying His rest is
dependent upon us learning His ways.

> Take My yoke upon you and learn of Me, for I am gentle
> (meek) and humble (lowly) in heart, and you will find
> rest (relief and ease and refreshment and recreation and
> blessed quiet) for your souls (Matthew 11:29).

I would like to suggest that you stop for a little bit and go over
and over these two Scriptures and think about the depth of what
Jesus is saying to you. There is rest for your soul! Peace—in your
mind, your emotions, and your will—is available.

I don't always follow my own advice, and recently I let myself
get upset and worried over a situation. I was only a few hours
away from getting ready to minister at an event, and that is the
worst time for me to get upset, but I did. A situation wasn't han-
dled properly that was going to affect me adversely, and I was the

only one at that point who could handle it. But if I was honest with myself—which is not always easy—I would have realized that although it was a responsibility I could not ignore, I didn't have to take care of it right that minute. I ended up getting myself on edge before I needed to teach in a big conference, and although God was merciful to me and it turned out well for the people, I forfeited the usual peace and comfort that I am accustomed to when I minister. It was more difficult for me to teach and easier for me to think my message wasn't very good. I kept looking at the clock, wanting my time to be up, and when I can't wait to be done, I know I have a problem.

I wanted to share this with you because it is important that you realize that no matter who you are or how much progress you have made, you will sometimes let yourself fall back into old patterns. It seems this is especially true with our thoughts and emotions. Always remember that God is merciful, and whatever mistakes you make, they are not a surprise or a shock to Him. He already knew what you would do before you did it, and He loves you anyway. With God there is always an opportunity for a new beginning or a fresh start!

Believe God's Promises

The book of Hebrews says that it is through believing that we can enter the rest of God (Hebrews 4:3, 10). When we put our faith, trust, and reliance on God and His promises to us, we begin to experience a healthy soul.

The will of man is part of the soul, and we need to use our free will to choose the will of God. If, for example, God's Word tells us not to do something and we do it anyway, we won't have rest in our souls until we have repented and received God's forgiveness.

Self-will and God's rest do not work together. God wants us to truly believe what He says, because when we do, then we will obey Him. When that happens, we will have rest for our souls. I think it is safe to say that we all begin our journey with God full of self-will, and trading that for God's will takes a lot of time and is often painful to us. Spiritual babies are no different than human babies. Both want their own way and will behave badly when they don't get it. Just as we train our children, God trains us.

> *Self-will and God's rest do not work together.*

If you have need of healing for a wounded soul, please believe me when I say that I know from experience that God's way is the best way to go. I have learned to yield to God's will over a period of years and I am actually still learning to let go of some things, but each time I trust God enough to do what He says, my life gets a little better. My soul enjoys more rest.

Believing (trusting God) is the only doorway into the rest of God. The more we trust God, the easier life becomes because we find that what we commit to Him, He does take care of. He may not do it in our timing or the way we would have, but He does and always will take care of us because He loves us unconditionally.

> *Make a decision right now to believe God more than you believe how you feel, what you want, or what you think.*

Make a decision right now to believe God more than you believe how you feel, what you want, or what you think. His promises are greater and more worthy of our trust than anything else. All else is shifting sand, but His Word is lasting and endures forever.

We are all building a life, and the foundation we build it on is even more important than the foundation we build our home on.

What foundation are you building your life on? Is it what popular opinion is, or what you think and feel, or what people will agree with? If it's any of those things, you are building on unstable ground. Jesus told a parable to make this point.

> So everyone who hears these words of Mine and acts upon them [obeying them] will be like a sensible (prudent, practical, wise) man who built his house upon the rock.
>
> And the rain fell and the floods came and the winds blew and beat against the house; yet it did not fall, because it had been founded on the rock.
>
> And everyone who hears these words of Mine and does not do them will be like a stupid (foolish) man who built his house upon the sand.
>
> And the rain fell and the floods came and the winds blew and beat against that house, and it fell—and great *and* complete was the fall of it (Matthew 7:24–27).

These Scriptures say the rain and floods come either way, whether we build on Jesus the Rock or on sinking sand. No one can avoid the trials and tribulations of life, but people who have built their life on the right foundation (Jesus) will come through the storms and still be standing strong.

Change Your Mind

If you want a change in your life, you will need to change your mind. Our thoughts have an amazing effect on us. The apostle Paul teaches that God has a wonderful plan for our lives, but in order to see it happen, we must have our minds completely renewed.

> Do not be conformed to this world, but be transformed by the renewal of your mind, that by testing you may discern what is the will of God, what is good and acceptable and perfect (Romans 12:2 ESV).

If you have a wounded soul, I am sure that a lot of your thinking is not yet in agreement with God's Word. Probably more than any other thing, Satan uses our thoughts to try to control us. He can suggest thoughts to us just as he did to Eve, but we don't have to receive them and take them as our own. However, we will if we don't know that they are lies intended to keep us in bondage.

I mentioned earlier that I thought because I had been sexually abused I would always have a second-rate life. I thought it was true because that was all I knew to think. But when I found out that God said I could let go of my past and enjoy a wonderful future, I realized my wrong thinking was keeping me in bondage, and yours will do the same thing to you.

In further chapters, I will be revealing the many lies that Satan uses to keep us bound to our past pain, and I believe that once you see the truth, it will make you free!

CHAPTER 5

Help Me! I Don't Understand Myself

The most difficult thing in life is to know yourself.

—Thales

Has anyone ever said to you, "I don't understand you at all!" I have heard that many times in my life and was unable to give any good answer because the truth was that I did not understand myself, either. Do you do things and wonder why you did them, or behave in certain ways, perhaps even repetitively, and then wonder why? How about things that you say? Do you blurt out words that hurt others and yet you are not even sure why you said them? You and I may not know why we do everything we do, but there is a reason.

Learning to understand the root of our behaviors is vital to changing them. Studying God's Word helps us gain insight. It may reveal to us that we have a root of fear in our lives that is affecting our actions and reactions. I grew up rooted in fear and had to learn that it was affecting me adversely, especially in relationships. My personality is quite bold, so it was difficult for me to face that many of my reactions to people and some situations were rooted in fear. Very few people

> *Learning to understand the root of our behaviors is vital to changing them.*

like to admit they are afraid, but aggressive, bold people like me really don't like to admit it because it tends to make us feel weak and out of control.

Still today I may have a strange reaction to something, and if I stop and ask God to show me why I said what I did or behaved the way I did, He often shows me that the source was fear. But I can react differently now than I did in the beginning of my journey toward the healing of my soul. Now I know that even when I am afraid, I can put my trust in God. We don't have to *be* afraid just because we *feel* afraid.

Fear is one of the main torments that the devil uses against people. His desire is to control us with it and prevent us from being the person God wants us to be. King David said that when he was afraid, he put his trust in God (Psalm 56:3). He was a man who had a wonderful relationship with God, and he was a king with great power and authority, and yet at times he experienced fear. Fear presents itself to everyone, but we don't need to let it control us.

Some of my unhealthy reactions were rooted in insecurity, feeling that I didn't fit in or that something was wrong with me, and the fear of being rejected. The fear of being taken advantage of was huge in my life, and it caused me to either not let people into my life or, if I did let them in, try to maintain control in every situation.

I recommend that when you have a bad or unusual reaction to a person or situation, instead of rushing past it, take time to ponder it and ask God to help you understand why you behaved as you did. Doing this has greatly helped me to get to the root of problems in my life.

Discernment

In the Christian context, discernment is perception with a view to spiritual direction and understanding.[15] A more practical definition would be to see beyond the way things appear to the way they truly are. I believe we need to understand ourselves, and that requires taking the time to see the motive behind our behaviors rather than merely the behavior itself.

Recently, I had a wrong attitude in a situation. It was not even one that I displayed, but in my heart, I knew my attitude wasn't what God would approve of, so I stopped and asked God to show me why I felt the way I did. Within a few moments, I heard the word *jealousy* in my heart. At first I didn't want to believe that I was jealous of someone, but I faced that it was true and asked God to help me grow up so I wouldn't have that kind of attitude. I did not feel condemned by what I saw, but I was actually relieved that I saw it. Always remember that you cannot do anything about something if you are blind to it. Don't be afraid to walk in the light with God and let Him reveal truth to you.

> For You have delivered my life from death, yes, and my feet from falling, that I may walk before God in the light of life *and* of the living (Psalm 56:13).

If we don't face truth, we will not be free from the things that steal our peace and joy. Discernment requires that we slow down and think more deeply in order to get to the root of our behaviors. Finding out why we do what we do is very valuable. Sometimes

Don't be afraid to walk in the light with God.

it takes a crisis to wake us up and help us see in ourselves what others see.

My behavior was not good for many years due to abuse I suffered in my childhood. After Dave and I had been married for about seven years, one morning he was getting ready for work and I was being very rude and disrespectful to him about something he wanted to do. That kind of behavior was not unusual for me, but on that morning he had reached the limit of what he was willing to endure, and he said, "Joyce, it is a good thing that I don't base my worth as a man on how you treat me and talk to me. If you continue to behave this way, I am not sure what I will do in the future." Having said that, he went to work. That was a crisis point for me, because Dave was not a man who made idle threats. We had three children, and I did love Dave. I didn't want him to leave me, so I decided to really make an effort to change.

I don't recommend trying to change without asking God for help, because without it you won't be successful. We need to let the Holy Spirit lead because He is our teacher and our guide. I asked God for help and He began to put resources in my hands that started giving me discernment, or insight, into the root of my problems.

One thing that was extremely helpful to me was reading books on the various personalities that people have. I was amazed at the insight I gained not only about myself but about others as well. I highly recommend that you take time to read some material along these lines and even take a personality test. Many of these types of tests are available online, and I think it may aid you in understanding yourself and in your journey toward healing.

When we talk about healing the brokenhearted, I think we are talking about healing those broken in personality. Personality is a combination of the natural temperament we are born with

combined with things that happen to us, especially in our forma-
tive years. I am a type A, or a choleric personality, according to
the test I took. The traits of that personality type explained me
perfectly and were very helpful to me.

The first book I read was about a Spirit-led personality by Tim
LaHaye. (He now has updated books available on the subject.)
His book revealed to me that although I had a temperament I was
born with, which included weaknesses and strengths, I could
learn to be Spirit-led in my responses to people and life.

One of the weaknesses of my temperament is a desire to control people and things. The choleric person is a leader; they are
happy to take control of any situation and tell others what to do.
I had to learn that this trait is good if I am in charge of something and need to lead, but it is not good if I use it to try to control things that are not my business. It has been interesting to
learn that many of our greatest strengths can also be some of our
greatest weaknesses, unless we learn to follow God's principles
throughout our life.

Learn all you can about yourself and it will help you become
your true self. I think we all have a
pretend self, one that we project to
the world, but God wants us to be
our true self, the person He created
us to be.

> *Learning all you can about
> yourself will help you become
> your true self.*

You don't have to wait for a crisis in your life to begin your
journey of healing and wholeness. The sooner you begin, the
happier you will be.

I recently spoke with a professional counselor in preparation to
write this book and asked her how she goes about helping people
with wounded souls. She said the first thing she has been taught
to do is give them a personality test. It was interesting to me that

although I did not get professional counseling, the Holy Spirit guided me to the same thing a counselor might have.

Finding Your Path

There are many different roads that can lead us to the same destination when it comes to healing our souls. We don't all have to take the same path in order to find the healing we need. Because we are individuals, God will lead us individually. But I want to make some suggestions that may help you. Some of them are negotiable and some are nonnegotiable.

The first thing that will help bring healing in our lives is a personal relationship with God and a diligent lifetime study of His Word. This is nonnegotiable. In my opinion, anyone seeking a healthy soul will only be able to find it in God's Word and with His help.

I recommend reading as often as you can. Read books that are based on biblical principles and those by Christian psychiatrists and psychologists. I prefer Christian authors because they usually present their material from a godly perspective. There are, of course, other authors that you can learn a lot from, but it is wise to be careful what you take into your soul. Just because something is written in a book does not make it true. I have read a lot of books on emotional healing, and much of what I learned has been extremely helpful to me, but occasionally I read something that simply did not agree with God's Word. Thankfully, I knew not to follow that advice.

You might need or choose to get counseling from a professional or a spiritual leader you respect. In both instances I think it is best to get a good recommendation from someone before beginning. Therapy is helpful to a lot of people because it gives them a chance to talk about their feelings and begin to understand what those feelings are rooted in. But if you don't want to do that or cannot find the right person, there is no need to think you will miss out. God will give you what you need and lead you to the things that will help you, just like He did me.

People are helped in different ways. One of the women I talked to while preparing for this book is one whose husband was addicted to pornography. Although he is a Christian, he was introduced to pornography in his childhood and had never been able to get free from it. This was, of course, devastating to my friend, and when I asked her what seemed to help her the most she replied, "Empathy." She said knowing that Jesus truly understood what she was going through was a major source of comfort to her. She also knew another woman who had experienced the same thing in her marriage, and talking with her, knowing the woman had true empathy for her, comforted her.

I also spoke with a woman whose husband had PTSD after serving in Afghanistan and receiving a brain injury as a result of a bombing. She said they were going through great difficulties in their marriage until they met a couple who had experienced very similar things and had found ways to work through their problems. She said that the couple was an absolute gift from God because they understood what they were going through and actually helped them to understand it better.

Many people can try to understand our pain, but no one understands it better than someone who has experienced what we're going through. I can have great empathy for someone who was sexually abused, has had cancer, was divorced due to infidelity, or has experienced many other things, but since I have never had substance addiction, I cannot truly know what someone goes through who is dealing with it.

Talk to someone. It doesn't have to be a counselor, but simply exposing the past to someone you trust will steal its power over you. Sadly, we often keep our pain a secret, and it festers in our souls until we become truly dysfunctional.

Being dysfunctional doesn't mean that we don't function in the world we live in, but it does mean that we don't function properly. I kept the sexual abuse in my childhood a secret and it was one of the things that kept me in bondage. I never told anyone except my mother until I married Dave when I was twenty-three years old. The fear of someone knowing what had been done to me was ruling my thoughts and actions and causing me to behave in ways that were dysfunctional. Although I had told my mother what my father was doing to me when I was nine years old, she chose not to believe me, so I thought no one else would, either.

We may think that people will reject us, blame us, or judge us harshly if they know our past, but if they do, then they have bigger problems than we do. If you had one disappointing experience, don't let that disappointment hold you in bondage to secrets that are making you sick. Find someone to talk to. Of course, Jesus is always available, and He completely understands and has compassion for you.

I also want to encourage you to be patient. Some of our problems leave a complicated mess in our souls that takes time to unravel. Healing usually comes in varying degrees, a little at a time. That has certainly been the case with me. God is rarely in a hurry because He is more interested in doing what needs to be done the right way, rather than doing it quickly. Being in a relationship with God will be very frustrating if we are extremely impatient, because His promises are received through faith and patience.

Don't ever give up! Don't get weary of doing what is right and you will reap a harvest in due time (Galatians 6:9).

Be a person of action, always ready to promptly do what God shows you to do. Knowing what to do but not doing it will not help you. You can get a prescription for medicine filled, but if you never take the medicine, it will not help you.

Be a lifetime learner, especially about yourself. There is an amazing person inside of you waiting to come out!

> *There is an amazing person inside of you waiting to come out!*

CHAPTER 6

You Are God's Beloved

*Beloved, now we are children of God; and it has not yet
been revealed what we shall be, but we know that when He
is revealed, we shall be like Him, for we shall see Him as
He is.*

—1 John 3:2 NKJV

Unconditional love is what people desire. The greatest happiness
in life is to know that we are loved for ourselves or perhaps in
spite of ourselves. God created us to be loved, and without that
love we don't function well. In my opinion, no person, no matter how good and kind they are, is capable of giving us love that
is totally unconditional. Only God can do that. If I said to you,
"God loves you at this moment in time as much as He ever will,"
what would you think?

I often say that to those attending my conferences, and I can
see from the puzzled and doubtful looks on their faces that they
are not sure they believe that. For most of us, the idea of unconditional love just doesn't fit into our ideology. But as I go on to
explain that God doesn't love us based on what we do but on who
He is, they begin to understand. However, it still takes a while
for me to convince people that they cannot do anything to earn
God's love. It is a free gift and can only be received by faith.

The apostle John tells us to put faith in the love that God has for us (1 John 4:16). We receive it first totally by faith, but eventually if we persist in believing it, we will begin to feel loved. The concept of anything good being ours without us needing to do something to earn it is very foreign

> *We are God's beloved.*

to us. Not only does God love us, but we are His beloved.

What does it mean to be the beloved of God? It is a term of affection and endearment, and it means to long for, to respect and hold in affectionate regard. As I pondered the word *beloved*, I sensed that it means to be loved or the thought of being loved at every moment in time. Just think about it: You are being loved right now and at every moment. There never has been and never will be a moment in time when you are not being perfectly loved.

I suggest you stop reading, close your eyes, and let your soul get quiet. Now say out loud, "I am God's beloved." Say it a few times and let it impact your soul. I believe this exercise could be very impacting, especially if you have never really believed that you are loved or have felt loved.

God the Father referred to Jesus as His Beloved Son, in whom He was well pleased (Matthew 3:17). The psalmist David's name means the beloved of God. Daniel was referred to three times by angels as God's beloved, and Paul at times referred to the New Testament believers as beloved. Also, the apostle John referred to himself as the beloved disciple, or the disciple whom Jesus loved. Surely John was a man who enjoyed a deep revelation of God's love for him and was bold enough to say so. What confidence he must have had!

Not only does God's love bring healing to our wounded souls, but it also gives us confidence and courage. The apostle John said that perfect love casts out fear, and that if we still have fear, then we have not reached the full maturity of God's love.

There is no fear in love [dread does not exist], but full-grown (complete, perfect) love turns fear out of doors *and* expels every trace of terror! For fear brings with it the thought of punishment, and [so] he who is afraid has not reached the full maturity of love [is not yet grown into love's complete perfection] (1 John 4:18).

I can remember reading this Scripture as a young believer and totally misunderstanding it. I thought it meant that if I could love others perfectly, I would have no fear in my life. I tried very hard to love others but seemed to always fail and revert back to selfishness. Eventually, I learned that before I could love anyone else, I had to receive the perfect love of God that was being offered to me and learn to love myself, and only then would I be able to love anyone else properly.

When we receive and enjoy the love of God, we are no longer afraid to let people into our lives and to give ourselves to them. We can love without reservation because we don't live with the fear of being taken advantage of. The perfect love of God casts out fear.

Don't be discouraged if it takes a while for you to fully grasp the thought of being loved unconditionally by God. Our experience has taught us that love seems to ebb and flow based on the moods of people and whether or not we are giving them what they want from us. We quickly fall into a pattern of trying to earn love by making people happy and fearing that love may be lost if we don't please them. People love us imperfectly, but God's love is perfect because He is perfect. He is love, and therefore it is impossible for Him to ever do anything less than love us unconditionally.

> *God's love is perfect because He is perfect.*

The more we fellowship with Jesus and learn about His character, experiencing His goodness, grace, and mercy in our lives, the more deeply we recognize His amazing love. Our souls may be so deeply wounded that we need to bask in the love of God for a long, long time to even begin sensing its healing effect. Deep wounds take time to heal, so be patient.

Tell Them I Love Them

For five years I taught a Bible study each Tuesday evening in my home. Eventually I was invited to teach a Bible study at my church on Thursday mornings. I refer to that as my first public speaking opportunity, and I really wanted it to be amazingly good. I prayed diligently about what the Lord wanted me to teach, and I continued to feel He wanted me to tell people how much He loves them. I must admit I resisted at first, telling the Lord that everyone knows that He loves them. After all, that is something many of us sing about as children: "Jesus loves me this I know, for the Bible tells me so."

The Lord was very clear that He did want me to tell them He loves them, stating that if people knew how much He loves them, they would not be tormented by fear. In obedience, I taught on God's love, and the message was received in an amazing way. It became obvious to me that not only did people need that revelation, but I also needed it myself. We can tell others that God loves them and still lack revelation about His love for us.

As I was preparing to teach others about how much God loves them, I discovered that I needed the same message. I did believe that God loves me, but I had to admit that I believed His love for me was conditional. Over the years, my faith in His love grew and grew, but even now I have to remind myself often that God doesn't stop loving me when I don't behave perfectly.

As I diligently studied and meditated on what the Bible teaches about how much God loves us and learned to watch for His love in my life, I finally began to feel loved. It was a beginning, but certainly not the end of my journey. I thought about God's love. I kept a notebook with every Scripture I could find on God's love written in it. I read any books I could find on God's love, and I confessed out loud in my prayer time that God loves me. You may be so convinced that you are unlovable that it will take the same type of diligence for you to really get a revelation of God's love for you. Receiving love seems to be especially difficult for those of us who have been deeply wounded in our lives, but once we begin to receive God's love, we find that love is the healing balm our souls need.

The apostle Paul knew the importance of people knowing that God loves them. He said,

> May Christ through your faith [actually] dwell (settle down, abide, make His permanent home) in your hearts! May you be rooted deep in love and founded securely on love (Ephesians 3:17).

I want to stress that Paul encouraged the believers to be rooted *deep* in God's love. Any tree that has deep roots will not fall or be destroyed during the storms it encounters, and when we have a deep revelation of God's love for us, it enables us to stand firm through the trials of life.

There are many things that happen to us that are not fair and are painful, and it is often tempting to revert to old ways during those times and begin to think that God does not love us or that He is not with us, but that is absolutely not true.

God is watching over everything in our lives, and if we trust Him through our difficulties, we will eventually see that He works them all out for our good (Romans 8:28).

Paul went on to pray that the believers would *experience* the love of God for themselves (Ephesians 3:18). That thought caught my attention as well as another one that is found in 1 John 4:16, instructing us to understand, recognize, and be conscious of God's love by observation. These two verses, when considered together, are encouraging us to watch for God's love in our lives because it can be seen and experienced in many different ways.

This exercise has been a source of great joy to me personally over the years. I have trained myself to watch for God's love, not taking any blessing in my life as coincidence, not even the tiny ones. This is one way I have found that I can be childlike in my daily relationship with my Lord. Not long ago I was thinking about a certain friend, and my thoughts were something like this: *She never really tells me that she loves me or asks me to spend any time with her.* Within a couple of days, I received this text message from her: "I love you!" A day or two after that I learned that she had planned to ask me to go to lunch but I had already planned something else. I took both of these events as "winks" from God, just His way of saying to me, "Joyce, I know your needs; as you delight yourself in Me, I will give you the desires of your heart" (Psalm 37:4).

This is just one example of many things like this that I believe happen to all of us, but unless we are looking for them and recognize them as signs of God's love, we will miss them. Does this sound foolish to you? Perhaps you are thinking, *Joyce, God has more important things to do than make sure you get a text from someone, just because you were wondering how a person felt about you.* Perhaps this type of relationship with God sounds childish to you, but Jesus did say that we should come to Him like little children (Matthew 18:3).

I lost my childhood to sexual abuse, violence, and fear. I never truly had an opportunity to be a carefree, trusting child, but God is a God of restoration, and He gives us back what the enemy has taken. Learn to approach your relationship with God as a little child, trusting Him, and depending on Him for everything.

> *God gives us back what the enemy has taken.*

The first book I wrote consisted of only a few pages. The title is *Tell Them I Love Them.* The book has been translated into close to one hundred languages, and God continues to use it today. It is a very simple version of what I am sharing with you in this chapter. I have since written many books, and I believe they all include some teaching about how much God loves us. It is not because I can't find anything new to say, but because nothing else will ever satisfy us unless we learn to receive God's unconditional love and realize that we are God's beloved.

Learn to Receive

You might think, *But why would God love me?* He loves you because He chooses to. He wants to. God loves us in order to satisfy His own intense desire. God is Love, and love needs to pour itself out; it must find someone to shower itself on. It cannot remain dormant because it is a living force. God sent His Son to die for us and pay for our sins because of and in order to satisfy the great and wonderful intense love He has for us (Ephesians 2:4–5). Neither you nor I will be able to find any viable reason why God loves us, but the truth is that He does, and it is up to us to either receive His love by faith or continue living empty, unfulfilling, and broken lives. To *receive* means to become as a receptacle and take in what is being offered. Can you do that today? Will you open your wounded soul and simply breathe in the love of God that is being poured out upon you right now? You are the beloved—you are being loved at this very moment.

We miss out on so much in our relationship with God because we try to "get" what He wants us to have instead of simply receiving it by faith. To *get* means you obtain something by struggle and effort. We cannot "get" God to love us because He already does, and He always will. He declares that He loves you with an everlasting love (Jeremiah 31:3). That is a love that cannot come to an end. So please believe in and receive God's love, and on those days when you make huge mistakes or have big problems and Satan, the enemy of your soul, tries to separate you from God's love, open up your Bible and read these verses:

> Who shall ever separate us from Christ's love? Shall suffering *and* affliction *and* tribulation? Or calamity *and* distress? Or persecution or hunger or destitution or peril or sword? (Romans 8:35).
>
> For I am persuaded beyond doubt (am sure) that neither death nor life, nor angels nor principalities, nor things impending *and* threatening nor things to come, nor powers,
>
> Nor height nor depth, nor anything else in all creation will be able to separate us from the love of God which is in Christ Jesus our Lord (Romans 8:38–39).

Whatever has happened in your life that has left you wounded and brokenhearted, it does not need to continue tormenting you.

God says in His Word that He has loved your life back from the pit of corruption and nothingness (Isaiah 38:17). Jesus was sent to heal the brokenhearted, to bind up their wounds and heal their bruises (Isaiah 61:1). Let His love begin to do the work in your wounded soul that it is intended to do!

CHAPTER 7

Hurting People Hurt People

Beloved, never avenge yourselves, but leave the way open for [God's] wrath; for it is written, Vengeance is Mine, I will repay (requite), says the Lord.

—Romans 12:19

On your journey of healing, possibly the most difficult thing that God will ask you to do is forgive the people who hurt you. It certainly was very challenging for me. One of the things that helped me a lot was when God showed me that hurting people hurt other people. We normally only think of how much we are hurting and then proceed to be angry with the people who have hurt us, but most of the time they are hurting, too.

Someone or something has hurt them, and they are acting out of their own pain, often not even realizing their actions are hurting others. My father finally told me when he was eighty years old that he was sorry for the sexual abuse in my childhood. He then went on to say, "I had no idea that what I was doing would hurt you so badly." In some ways that sounds preposterous. How could he not know he was hurting me? He did know that what he was doing was wrong, otherwise, he would not have told me over and over to never tell anyone. But he was so absorbed in his own lustful desires that he never even considered how his actions were impacting me.

I eventually discovered that my father had come from a family in which incest was not uncommon. When I was a young girl, his father (my grandfather) attempted to molest me, as did two of my uncles, so I know the traits of sexual abuse were present in the family. If you read the statistics I provide in appendix I, you will see that it is estimated that 1 million girls in America are victims of father-daughter incest. Sadly, it is more common than we realize.

My father was always bitter toward his father, and we never knew why, but it is easy to imagine what the root of his bitterness might have been. He was hurting, but he drowned his own pain in addictive behaviors, and I seriously doubt that he ever realized that his ungodly actions were the result of pain and possibly abuse in his own childhood.

My father was a very angry and bitter man, and if anyone ever made him really angry about anything, he was determined to never forgive. I learned that my father was violent toward my mother before they even got married, so it is reasonable to conclude he was angry and filled with rage at a very early age. She was seventeen when they married, and she stayed with him until he died at the age of eighty-three, but for many of their sixty-plus years of marriage, at various times he hit her, slapped her, and threatened her with beatings if she gave him any trouble at all.

My mother lived in fear of my father and cowered under his domineering personality. If she had been more courageous, she would have left him when I was a little girl and I originally told her about what he was doing to me. She could have prevented herself and my brother and me from being abused. But she wasn't courageous, and she stayed with him. She told me many years later that she simply did not think she could face the scandal, and she didn't think she could support herself and me and my brother. I was struck by the fact that it was her own thoughts that defeated her. She thought she couldn't, so she didn't.

Once I realized that my father was acting out of his own pain, as well as lust and greed, the idea of forgiving him became a little easier. That doesn't mean that he wasn't responsible for his actions, because he was, but continuing to despise him and be angry with him wasn't helping me, nor was it helping him to change. If you remain angry with someone who has hurt you, you are giving them permission to keep hurting you over and over again through your memories and bitterness.

I didn't forgive my father and my mother because it was easy, but because it is God's command that we do so. Scripture teaches us in multiple places that we must forgive our enemies and that God is our Vindicator.

I believe that for many women, hanging on to anger and refusing to forgive those who have hurt them stands in the way of their healing. We cannot go forward if we are bitterly hanging on to the past.

The Single Most Powerful Thing You Can Do

I believe that forgiving the people who hurt us is the single most powerful thing we will ever do. It releases us from emotional torment and frees us to get on with life. While the process of forgiveness is often difficult, when you make a decision to truly forgive and let go of the bitterness, anger and resentment you've had toward others, it will save you from years of misery. The question is, what

> When you make a decision to truly forgive, you can put an end to years of misery.

kind of life do you want to have: one that is free and enjoyable, or one that is bitter and keeps you tethered to the past?

It is very important for anyone reading this book who is in need of healing for a wounded soul to take this command from God seriously. Don't decide to rush past this chapter because you have already decided that you just can't forgive the people who hurt you because it is too hard. Forgiving our enemies is nonnegotiable for anyone who wants to enjoy the promise of God for restoration. It is something God teaches us to do, and it is something that Jesus modeled in His own life. Jesus prayed, while suffering on the cross, that His crucifiers would be forgiven. He knew that they were hurting Him out of their own hurt and confusion.

God is merciful, and mercy always looks beyond what someone did to why they did it. There is always a why. Because I was hurt, I made mistakes with my children and my husband. The devil's plan is for us to continue living with the pain of our past and to wound others, from generation to generation, preventing anyone from enjoying what Jesus died to give them. But Jesus gave us instructions about how we can defeat the devil and not have our history become our destiny.

Let It Go

In Matthew 6:12, Jesus taught that we should ask God to forgive our sins "as we also have forgiven (left, remitted, and let go of the debts, and have given up resentment against) our debtors." To forgive means to let go of something instead of holding on to it. The wounds and pain we hold on to become a heavy burden to carry, and we carry it constantly until we make the decision to let it go. Carrying these burdens can be the root cause of many mental and physical illnesses and disorders. We are not created by God to be burdened, but instead He invites us to let things go that burden us and trust Him to take care of us. We are to cast all of our care on Him. Here are two Scripture verses that have encouraged me often, and I hope they will minister to you also.

> Casting the whole of your care [all your anxieties, all your worries, all your concerns, once and for all] on Him, for He cares for you affectionately and cares about you watchfully (1 Peter 5:7).
>
> Cast your burden on the Lord [releasing the weight of it] and He will sustain you; He will never allow the [consistently] righteous to be moved (made to slip, fall, or fail) (Psalm 55:22).

Don't keep holding on to something that you cannot do anything about. If someone hurt you badly and you hang on to it mentally and emotionally, then you are allowing it to keep hurting you day after day. Help yourself and let it go! Of course, your mind screams, "It isn't fair," and it's not. There is nothing fair about forgiving someone for abusing or misusing you, but then again it wasn't fair for Jesus to die for our sins. God will never ask us to forgive anyone for more than He has forgiven us. A rattlesnake, if cornered, will sometimes become so angry it will bite itself. That is exactly what happens when we harbor hate and resentment against others—we "bite" and poison ourselves. We think that we are harming others by holding on to spite and hate, but the deeper harm is actually done to ourselves.

Forgiving someone who hurt us is never something we will feel like doing, but we can decide to do it, and God will help us. Release your enemies so God can begin to deal with them. Hopefully, like my father, they will eventually respond to His relentless love and let Him into their lives, but if they don't, sadly, they will end up reaping what they have sown.

Letting go involves making a commitment to stop thinking and talking about the things that people have done to you, unless, of course, you are receiving counseling or sharing your victory over it in order to help someone else. Sometimes people replay moments of betrayal, abuse, or rejection over and over in their minds, and whether they know it or not, doing so holds them in bondage to it. Our minds affect our emotions, and when we rehearse abusive events over and over, it brings back the original pain as if it were a current event.

God doesn't want us to live in captivity to our own bitterness or heartache. Instead, He longs for us to give these negative feelings to Him, forgive the ones who hurt us, and trust that He will work good out of what happened to us and bring us a double recompense for our former pain.

> Instead of your [former] shame you shall have a twofold recompense; instead of dishonor and reproach [your people] shall rejoice in their portion. Therefore in their land they shall possess double [what they had forfeited]; everlasting joy shall be theirs (Isaiah 61:7).

When we obey God, He always brings a reward. Letting go may be difficult, but looking forward to your reward will make it easier. Charlotte Brontë said in *Jane Eyre*, "Life appears to me too short to be spent in nursing animosity or registering wrongs." God may ask us to do difficult things, just as He asked His Son, who paid for our sins, but He will never ask us to do something without giving us the ability to do it.

When we obey God, He always brings a reward.

A great example of the power of forgiveness comes from the life of Nelson Mandela. A reporter shared this story:

> Mandela made a grand, elegant, dignified exit from prison and it was very, very powerful for the world to see. But as I was watching him walking down that dusty road, I wondered whether he was thinking about the last 27 years, whether he was angry all over again. Later, many years later, I had a chance to ask him. I said, "Come on, you were a great man, you invited your jailers to your inauguration, you put your pressures on the government. But tell me the truth. Weren't you really angry all over again?" And he said, "Yes, I was angry. And I was a little afraid. After all I'd not been free in so long. But," he said, "when I felt that anger well up inside of me, I realized that if I hated them after I got outside the gate, then they would still have me." And he smiled and said, "I wanted to be free, so I let it go."[16]

Bitterness starts out small. An offense burrows its way into our hearts. We replay it in our minds and it creates deep ruts that are often hard to build back up, but God will help us if we will ask Him to and then let Him take the lead. Letting God lead means that we follow His commands no matter how we feel about them. Everything He asks us to do is for our benefit and the benefit of those we are doing life with.

Repressed Anger and Secrets

Our secrets make us sick inside. They fester in our souls and seep out into our behavior. Sometimes we can tell that a person is angry because they are explosive when things don't go their way, but at other times we cannot see the anger directly. We often become good at hiding from our problems and repressing the anger we feel over our disappointing lives. At least we think we are hiding it, but in reality it is like a beach ball—we try to submerge it, but no matter how hard we try, it keeps popping up again and again. In some ways repressed anger is worse than expressed anger. At least if we are expressing anger, we know we are angry, but if we repress it and pretend we are fine when in reality we are not, the anger eats away at our souls in many ways that steal the quality of life we want to have.

Anger can manifest as depression, anxiety, mood disorders, eating disorders, alcoholism, drug addiction, violence, and many other things. There isn't much we can do with anger that makes any sense except to let it go, and that is exactly why God has instructed us to do so.

Perhaps it is time for you to get to the root cause of some of the problems that you deal with rather than merely continuing to treat symptoms that never completely go away. Getting to the root of our problems is what the healing of the soul is all about. We open ourselves up to God and let Him into all the areas of our lives, and we trust Him to guide us through the process of restoration and wholeness. When things are brought out into the light, they lose their power over us. The Bible says that when anything is exposed and reproved by the light, it is made visible and clear (Ephesians 5:13).

Making the decision to forgive your enemies is the first step, and when you do that you can begin to deal with the anger you have from the unjust things that have happened to you. We can let go of bitterness and anger and replace them with trust in God and hope for the future.

Pray for Your Enemies and Bless Them

Making a decision to forgive is the first step, but there is something else God instructs us to do that is an important part of forgiving. It is the instruction God gives for us to pray for and bless our enemies. *Wow! God, You have got to be kidding. How can I pray for someone to be blessed when the truth is that I don't want them to be blessed?* When we pray for our enemies to be blessed, we are releasing them so God can bless them with the truth that has the power to make them free from their abusive nature. We pray for God to open their eyes so they can know truth and receive Him as Savior and Lord.

I also believe God wants us to be open to helping those who have hurt us in a practical way when they need help. He gave me the grace to do this with my parents by having me help them with their daily needs for approximately fifteen years when they were elderly and needed help. It took a lot of time and money to do so, and I will admit that it was not something I enjoyed, but I knew it was the right thing to do, so I did it. I'll say it again: Forgiving your enemies is one of the most powerful things you can ever do. It opens the door to multiple blessings in your life, including peace, joy, and the recompense of God.

I forgave my parents and helped them in obedience to God, and although I didn't enjoy it, I did enjoy knowing that only God could enable me to do it and that I had finally won a victory over the devil. God blessed my obedience, and the result is that the devil would not ever be successful in bringing back the pain of the past into my life.

According to God's Word, we overcome evil with good (Romans 12:21). The evil things that were done to you can be overcome by a willingness to let go of bitterness and anger and by praying for and blessing your enemies. It may seem that you are just helping them, but in reality, you are helping yourself. When we forgive and then pray for and bless our enemies, the Word of God states that we are behaving as our Father in heaven would. I want to leave you with two Scripture verses I have had to read and meditate on hundreds of times. They have helped me do the things I am teaching in this chapter and I pray they will help you also.

> Invoke blessings upon *and* pray for the happiness of those who curse you, implore God's blessing (favor) upon those who abuse you [who revile, reproach, disparage, and high-handedly misuse you] (Luke 6:28).
>
> But love your enemies and be kind *and* do good [doing favors so that someone derives benefit from them] and lend, expecting *and* hoping for nothing in return *but* considering nothing as lost *and* despairing of no one; and then your recompense (your reward) will be great (rich, strong, intense, and abundant), and you will be sons of the Most High, for He is kind *and* charitable *and* good to the ungrateful *and* the selfish and wicked (Luke 6:35).

May these verses strengthen you and enable you to forgive anyone who has or ever will hurt you.

CHAPTER 8

Unload the Guilt and Shame

Fear not, for you shall not be ashamed; neither be confounded and depressed, for you shall not be put to shame. For you shall forget the shame of your youth, and you shall not [seriously] remember the reproach of your widowhood any more.

—Isaiah 54:4

Guilt and shame: two of the most tormenting, destructive, and debilitating things that wounded people experience. But God promises us complete deliverance and freedom from both of them. Guilt and shame create a burden that pressures us. Our days are absorbed with feeling bad about ourselves for what we have done wrong or what has been done to us.

The devil screams his lies into our minds: *What happened to you is your fault. If you had been better, you would not have been beaten. If you had been stronger, you would not have allowed your father to sexually abuse you. If you had not been such a coward, you would have stood up to your abuser instead of cowering to their threats. If you were smarter, you would not have been rejected. If you were prettier, you would have been chosen. If you had been more careful, your child would not be dead. If you had caught the symptoms sooner and gone to the doctor, you wouldn't be facing chemo.* But I want to tell you today that it is not your fault.

People don't abuse you, misuse you, or even mistreat you because there is something wrong with you; they do it because there is something wrong with them. They hurt us because they are hurting. Broken and wounded people absolutely cannot recover until they unload the guilt and shame that they carry.

> *Broken people absolutely cannot recover until they unload the guilt and shame that they carry.*

We have all made mistakes in life, and we have all done things that we are ashamed of, but being ashamed of something we have done, or even something that was done to us, is totally different than internalizing the shame and becoming ashamed of ourselves. The feelings of shame my mother carried about the incest in our family were the reason she never confronted and exposed it. Sadly for her, she internalized it, and even at the age of eighty-nine, right before she died, I heard her say what she had said so many times: "I know you blame me for what your father did to you!" Although I had forgiven her many years previously, she never stopped feeling guilty. She never forgave herself.

How much better it would have been for all of us, including my father, if she had faced the problem head-on and dealt with it. But instead, she took what seemed to her at the time to be the easy path, and it ended up being the hardest path in the end because it was something she was never able to recover from. Running from our problems never works because somehow they seem to be able to outrun us. The way to overcome them is to confront them with God's help.

My mother ended up with mental illness that I will always believe stemmed from the shame and guilt she felt over the choices she made. It wasn't her fault that my father did what he did, but it was her responsibility to confront it. When we run from our responsibilities and don't do what we know we should do, the results become impossible to run away from. You cannot let go of the past until you deal with it.

If you are loaded down with guilt and shame, it is time for you to take a stand and draw a line in the sand, so to speak, and refuse to continue the way you have been living. If you have things in the past that you are sorry for, then repent and receive your forgiveness from God and get on with your life. If you have been abused in any way, then forgive those who hurt you and get on with your life. But don't continue merely feeling guilty and ashamed. It is time for a new beginning. Your past does not have any power over your present moment unless you allow it to.

Guilt is anger that is directed at ourselves. We are angry with ourselves because of what we did or something that happened to us. Even though our guilt has been removed by the grace of God, we will still suffer with it until we forgive ourselves. When we begin a new life with Christ, all things from the past are finished, and a new life awaits us. But if we let him, Satan will continue making us feel guilty. It is his way of holding us in bondage, and the

> *Guilt is anger that is directed at ourselves.*

guilt steals all of the energy God has given us to live life as He meant it to be lived. A constant feeling of guilt leaves us tired and can even make us physically ill.

Guilt Two Ways

There are only two ways that guilt can settle in your soul and torment you. The first is if you have done something wrong and never asked for forgiveness, and the second is if you have asked for but not received the mercy and forgiveness that God offers us. When sin is forgiven, it is removed as far as east is from west (Psalm 103:12) and there is nothing left to feel guilty about; therefore, any feelings of guilt should be resisted. The feeling may be real, but it is based on a lie, not a reality. When God forgives us, He remembers our sin no more (Isaiah 43:25), and surely, if He can forget our wrongdoing, then we can, too. The Bible is very clear that Jesus took our transgression and guilt upon Himself, and since He took them, we don't have them any longer.

> But He was wounded for our transgressions, He was bruised for our guilt *and* iniquities; the chastisement [needful to obtain] peace *and* well-being for us was upon Him, and with the stripes [that wounded] Him we are healed *and* made whole (Isaiah 53:5).

This Scripture is one of the most powerful we find in God's Word. Jesus took our pain, sins, and guilt and allowed Himself to be wounded for our wounds. And then the promise comes: Through the sacrifice He made, we are healed and made whole. It is already done.

We may also feel guilty for something that someone else did to us. We think we should have or could have done something to prevent their actions. For example, many children feel that if they had been better behaved, their parents would not have divorced. This type of thinking is wrong, of course, but nonetheless it is tormenting and destructive. I had a recording playing in my head for years that went like this: *What is wrong with me? What is wrong with me? What is wrong with me? What am I doing that makes my father want to do this to me?*

I was convinced that something was wrong with *me*, and

that was the reason my father wanted to use me to vent his lust, instead of receiving and loving me as his daughter.

People who have wounded souls may suffer deeply with feeling that something is wrong with them, as well as feeling guilty and ashamed. But God can deliver them! If you are one of those people, please be assured that not only can God deliver you, but He *wants* to deliver you. My freedom was not instantaneous, and yours may not be either, but as I continued to renew my mind with God's Word, my feelings began to change, gradually but surely, and the same thing will happen for you. Let me say again, if someone abused, rejected, or abandoned you, it was not your fault. It is time to stand up for yourself and stop allowing the lies of the enemy to control your destiny.

> *If you were abused, rejected, or abandoned, it was not your fault.*

Satan seeks to make us feel worthless and devalued, and the best way to do that is to load us down with false guilt and toxic shame. To feel ashamed of something we did wrong, or even of something wrong that was done to us, is not surprising; it is actually quite normal. But to feel ashamed of ourselves because of what happened takes shame and guilt to a dangerous level that begins to poison all areas of our life. It is time to be free from shame!

Dealing with Shame

Feeling shame means to be confounded, confused, dry, disappointed, or stopped. The word *confounded* means ashamed, confused, defeated, or overthrown. It also means to be damned, and that means doomed to punishment. This describes many of the problems we encounter when we go through life with a wounded soul that needs to be healed. Nothing seems to work out for us, we feel dry and lifeless, confusion is our companion, we often have difficulty making decisions, and life in general is very disappointing.

I tried many different remedies for these maladies, but I didn't get any real help until God showed me through a book I read that at the core of my being, I was ashamed of who I was. Shame had poisoned my thoughts, emotions, and life choices. Dry and disappointed is a good description of how I normally felt. I simply was not happy. The shame had to be dealt with, and it was through taking God at His word, instead of continuing to be controlled by my thoughts and emotions, that I was finally set free.

I learned about guilt and condemnation a long time before I even heard about the problem of shame. Of course, I was ashamed of what my father had done to me, and that was one of the major reasons I kept my past a secret for so long. I knew I was ashamed of what had been done to me, but I had no idea that I was ashamed of myself and who I was because of it. Once I saw this, many things began to fall into place for me. The shame that I had internalized and taken as my identity was preventing me from living the good life that Jesus died for me live.

I had always wondered what was wrong with me, and perhaps you have, too. But like everything else that is wrong in our life, Jesus has a remedy for our wrongness and our feelings of guilt and shame. He offers us rightness, or righteousness, and that means right standing with God (2 Corinthians 5:21). He takes our sin and gives us His righteousness. Did you know that you have been made the righteousness of God through your faith in Jesus?

Once I learned that I had rightness (righteousness), I spent several years learning how to let that truth become a reality in my life. The Bible says that we are to put on righteousness (Ephesians 6:14). To "put it on" means to firmly believe it and learn to walk with the dignity God offers you as His precious, valuable child. We are not righteous in and of ourselves, but we can, by faith, receive God's righteousness just as we would receive and enjoy any other gift that has been given to us. It is not God's will for you to feel bad about yourself, compare yourself with other people, and keep an ongoing record of everything you think is wrong with you. You can actually learn to accept and enjoy yourself, knowing that God meets us where we are and will help us get to where we need to be.

> *Learn to walk with the dignity God offers you as His precious child.*

The mere fact that you know a Scripture about right standing with God or have heard someone teach on righteousness with God does not mean that it has become a reality in your life. I often tell people that we really don't fully know or have revelation of any of God's truths until we can see that they are working in our lives. When you truly believe that you have been made right with God through faith in Christ, you will stop feeling guilty, condemned, and ashamed.

If you still suffer a lot with feelings of guilt and shame, you still need more revelation about who you are in Christ. No matter how long it takes, please don't get discouraged and give up. Giving up is exactly what Satan wants you to do, but God wants you to keep pressing into His truth. Continue studying about your right standing with God and confess it often, and the day will come when the reality of it will make its way from your head to your heart. Once it is firmly established in you, then although the devil may come against you, he will never defeat you.

After over forty years of studying and teaching God's Word, I still confess each day that I am the righteousness of God in Christ. Doing so reminds me of who I am in Jesus, and confessing His Word defends and protects me from the lies of Satan.

Even if you are not where you want to be in your walk with God, you don't have to feel guilty and ashamed. You can rejoice that you have made some progress. Jesus, who began a good work in you, will complete it. He will con-

God is working in you right now!

tinue developing and perfecting His work in us right up to the time of Christ's return (Philippians 1:6). When the devil attacks you with guilt and shame you can say, "I may not be where I need to be, but thank God, I am not where I used to be. God is working in me right now, and each day I am making more progress!"

How much time do you waste feeling bad about yourself and wondering what is wrong with you because you can't seem to behave in a way that society says is right and proper? Whatever amount of time it is, it is too much time. It is precious time wasted that you can never get back again. Learn to see yourself the way God sees you instead of how the world views you. The world may call you a victim, but God calls you victorious. The world calls you damaged goods, but God calls you His daughter.

I can promise you that if you receive Christ as your Savior and begin letting His Word renew your thinking, you will gradually feel better and better about yourself and that will enable you to finally enjoy your life. Learn to enjoy the progress you have made even if it seems tiny to you, instead of constantly thinking about how far you still have to go.

The Accuser

If you listen closely, you will frequently hear accusing thoughts bombarding your mind. Are you guilty of some wrongdoing simply because you have a thought that is accusing you of being wrong? Absolutely not! The devil is a liar, and the mind is the battlefield on which he tries to defeat us. Just as he lied to and deceived Eve in the Garden of Eden, he also lies to and attempts to deceive us. One of his main goals is to prevent us from loving and valuing ourselves. If he can be successful in that, then it's likely that he will be successful in controlling our lives through his lies.

The mind is the battlefield on which the devil tries to defeat us.

Satan is the accuser of God's children (Revelation 12:10). He brings accusation against us day and night, but we can defeat him by believing the promises of God more than we believe the thoughts that endlessly float through our minds. Please realize that every thought you have is not necessarily the truth. God's Word is truth.

We overcome Satan by the blood of Christ, the Word of God, and our testimony (Revelation 12:11). What is your testimony? Some of it may still be in the making, but part of it is that you are a redeemed, powerful child of God, who is filled with possibility and potential. You are actually a miracle in the making! While you were still in sin, Jesus died for you, so just imagine what He has planned now that you have been forgiven and have a desire to walk with Him. I can promise you that no matter how creative your imagination is, you still cannot fully imagine the amazing plan He has for your life.

We find out what God's plan is as we walk with Him day after day. I am continually stunned at what God has done in my life.

He has literally brought me from total misery and failure to being a happy, fulfilled, and productive person. Yes, it has been a long journey, and no, it hasn't been easy, but I wouldn't trade it for anything. On those days when pressing forward seems especially difficult, just remember that you are on your way to greater things!

Keep reminding yourself that the devil is a liar, and replace his lies with God's Word. Each time you do, you are winning a small battle that will eventually make you the victor in the war he has launched against your life.

You don't have to live with the torment of guilt and shame. You can enjoy right standing with God through Jesus—the reality that He has taken your guilt, shame, and blame. As a child of God who deeply desires to please Him, there will be times when you may feel ashamed of something you have done that is wrong, but those feelings can be promptly taken care of through repentance and receiving God's mercy.

CHAPTER 9

Finding Your True Self

Therefore, if anyone is in Christ, he is a new creation. The old has passed away; behold, the new has come.

—2 Corinthians 5:17 ESV

Not knowing who we truly are causes confusion, lack of fulfillment, and emotional misery. Many people create false identities and pretend to be something that they are not. For instance, if we are afraid to be vulnerable, we may develop a tough exterior to keep anyone from thinking we are weak or needy. The fear of what people think of us and craving their approval may cause us to alter our personalities in an effort to be whatever we think they want us to be instead of enjoying the freedom of being ourselves.

Chameleons are lizards that have an ability to change colors in order to blend into their surroundings. They do this to protect themselves from predators, and although we cannot change colors, we do sometimes develop false identities, hoping to protect ourselves from rejection or disapproval.

It is quite common for wounded people who fear rejection to become people pleasers, living their lives according to what other people think they should be and do instead of finding and becoming their true selves. We are never free until we are free to be ourselves.

We are never free until we are free to be ourselves.

The world pressures us to fit into a certain image they approve of. They tell us what to wear, how much to weigh, how to style our hair, the level of education we need to be savvy, how to behave in every situation—the list goes on and on. Without it always being said, we are well aware that if we don't fit into these molds and images, we will be unacceptable and, therefore, rejected. We often spend more time in relationships trying not to be rejected than we do building healthy connections.

When we receive Jesus as our Savior, according to Scripture, we are born again, or born anew. It is a point in our lives where we are invited to let go of anything old and fully become the amazing person that God originally intended us to be before our experience with the world and sin wounded us. Our sins are forgiven, and we have an opportunity to receive God's unconditional love and mercy. We are made new, and life is filled with possibility. I like to say that we become new spiritual clay, and by allowing the Holy Spirit to mold us, rather than letting the world do it, we can become our true selves.

Are You Tired of Hiding?

Pretending is just a form of hiding. We hide who we truly want to be and pretend to be something that we believe will protect us, or something that we think is expected of us. In *The Mask Behind the Mask*, biographer Peter Evans says that actor Peter Sellers played so many roles he sometimes was not sure of his own identity. Approached once by a fan who asked him, "Are you Peter Sellers?" Sellers answered briskly, "Not today," and walked on.[17]

Deep down inside, I always felt a little different than most other women, so I hid who I truly wanted to be and desperately tried to be like the other women around me. I tried to do what they did, thinking that would make me more acceptable. I had yet to realize that our true identity is not found in what we do, but in who we are as individuals. The kind of person we are is more important than what we do.

I tried to be softer and meeker because I knew and admired women who were that way. They seemed to glide through life more easily than I did. It seemed I was always fighting against something, trying to be tough and in charge, while these other women found it easy to sweetly go along with what others wanted to do. Thankfully, I now realize I wasn't created by God to follow but to lead, and because of that, I would not ever just go along with whatever was taking place. If something needed to be changed, I would be the first to step up and try to change it.

I was born to lead, but I definitely needed some Holy Spirit molding. He molds us into the image of Jesus Christ, and then we learn to let Jesus shine through our unique gifts and temperaments. I had a lot of what is often referred to as rough edges, and it took a lot of Holy Spirit sandpaper to smooth me out and make me easier to be with.

In an effort to be a "regular woman"—whatever that is—I also tried to learn to sew so I could make my family some of their clothes. I am sure they are still grateful that I was not successful at that venture. I talked my husband into planting a garden so I could be more like some of the women I knew who had gardens, but no matter how hard I tried to grow vegetables, they always died. God will not help us do something He has not gifted or asked us to do. Although sewing and gardening are admirable skills, they were not what God wanted me to do with my time, and for that reason He would not bless my efforts and make them successful.

The more I failed at these pursuits, the worse I felt about

myself. The destructive cycle of me trying to do things and failing continued until I learned to be courageous enough to be myself. All the trying and failing frustrated me, and, of course, I took those frustrations out on the people I loved the most: my family. I finally admitted to myself that I hated sewing and gardening, and when I started honestly asking myself what I did love and want to do, I realized that I loved to study the Bible and teach it. It was one giant step in becoming my true self.

God will never help you to be someone else. He has gifted you to be able to do something special, but it may not be what other people are doing. Take some time and search your heart to discover what you love, and then find the courage in Christ to do it. Even if what you desire to do is something that has never been done before, remember that there is always someone who is the first at everything.

> *God will never help you to be someone else.*

I had spent so much time in my life trying to be someone I wasn't and denying myself in the process that I no longer even knew what my own desires were. Who was I? What did I want to do? Where did I fit into God's grand plan?

When you find your true self, you find a place where you are comfortable with yourself. You easily function in the role you choose in life and you bear good fruit. Pretending to be something that you truly are not is like wearing clothes that are extremely tight fitting. You are in them, but you are never comfortable. Being yourself is like wearing your most comfy clothes and sitting in your favorite overstuffed chair. The only role you can ever be really comfortable with is the one where you play your true self.

Have you found your sweet spot in life? Are you comfortable

being you? How much do you compare yourself with others and perhaps try to become someone you are not? Asking these questions may be the beginning of finding your true self and becoming the you that God created you to be!

Self-Acceptance

We all crave acceptance, but the greatest need we have is to accept our unique selves. I have found that the more I have learned to accept myself, the more other people accept me, too. When we reject ourselves and waste our time trying to be someone that we are not, other people often reject us. The Bible does say that we get what we believe (Matthew 8:13) and our thoughts can become our reality (Proverbs 23:7).

We behave according to what we believe, and our behavior affects how other people feel about us. If we act confidently, it causes other people to put their confidence in us, too. But if we do not act confidently, it causes others to lack confidence in us. As an employer I have experienced both types of people.

I once had an executive assistant who was a lovely woman, but she lacked confidence, and eventually, I could not keep her in the position she was in because her lack of confidence prevented her from being able to do the job that I needed her to do. She had the ability, but she lacked the confidence to do it.

If you want people to have confidence in you, you must first have confidence in yourself. Theodore Roosevelt said, "Believe you can and you are halfway there."[18]

As a child of God, you can be confident in Christ, knowing that He is always with you and ready to help you do whatever you need to do in life.

Self-Rejection

Before you can accept yourself, you must stop rejecting yourself. Henri Nouwen, a well-known minister and author, admittedly struggled trying to find his true self, and he said, "Over the years, I have come to realize that the greatest trap in our life is not success, popularity, or power, but self-rejection."[19] He also said, "Self-rejection is the greatest enemy of the spiritual life because it contradicts the sacred voice that calls us the Beloved."[20]

Our true self is one who is the beloved of God. Every other identity is a false one. If we know we are God's beloved, it gives us confidence to step into our true destiny, whatever that may be. It may be to sew and grow a garden, or it may be to travel the world preaching the Gospel. But whatever our true destiny is, it isn't nearly as important as us being comfortable with what it is. In order to find healing for our souls, it is important to allow the Word of God to define us rather than allowing the world to define us. When our time in this world comes to an end, the only opinion that will matter is God's, so don't waste your life being overly concerned about what other people think of you.

The world places labels on people—wounded, abused, betrayed, divorced, rebel, victim, damaged, and so on. And far too many times, we allow the labels of the world to become our identity and begin to define us. Perhaps we believe what others have said about us because we have either not known or have forgotten what God says about us.

Here are a few Scriptures that give us an idea of how God views us:

> But you are a chosen race, a royal priesthood, a dedicated
> nation, [God's] own purchased, special people, that you

may set forth the wonderful deeds *and* display the virtues
and perfections of Him Who called you out of darkness
into His marvelous light (1 Peter 2:9).

Perhaps you are part of a race that has been rejected, but now
God says you are a chosen race, you're special, and He is going to
use you to display His wonderful deeds and perfections.

And set your minds *and* keep them set on what is above
(the higher things), not on the things that are on the earth.
For [as far as this world is concerned] you have died,
and your [new, real] life is hidden with Christ in God
(Colossians 3:2–3).

Do you see it? Your new real life is hidden with Christ in God!
You do have a real life, a true self, but it can only be found in
Christ. The birth of that true self occurs when you become a child
of God through the new birth (receiving Jesus as your Savior).

And put on the new nature (the regenerate self) created in
God's image, [Godlike] in true righteousness and holiness
(Ephesians 4:24).

Now, put on the new person that God is calling you to be. Step
out by faith in Him and shake off all the old labels. Call yourself
the Beloved of God, confident, accepted, and strong in Him.

Loss of Identity

Satan works hard to make sure either that we never know our
identity as God's beloved child or that somewhere along our

journey in life we lose the sense of that truth. It is equivalent to having amnesia. Dave and I occasionally talk about what it must be like for people who have amnesia. Just imagine waking up in a hospital, being told you were in an accident, and when asked your name, you have no idea who you are.

In *The Bourne Identity*, Matt Damon plays Jason Bourne—a special forces operative who has suffered amnesia and is trying to figure out who he really is. The fundamentals of his journey are not too different from our own.

In the mountains of Switzerland, Jason hitches a ride to Paris with a young woman named Marie. He's running from the police—but he's not even sure why. He tries to keep quiet about his situation until the frustration overwhelms him. Finally, in response to her asking a simple question, he turns to her and says desperately, "I don't know who I am or where I am going."

Jason Bourne had all the skills required to not be afraid of anyone or anything, but because he didn't know who he was, he functioned in fear and desperation. Does that describe you or someone you know? It certainly would have been a good description of me at one time in my life. I had spiritual amnesia—I didn't know who I was in God. I didn't know that I was His beloved.

So many of us are running from something, to somewhere— but it's impossible to know where we are going if we don't know who we are. God's fingerprints are all over our lives, and as we search Him out, the pieces begin to fall into place. Ultimately, we find our true self—our true identity—is only in Christ, and only then do we find out where we are going with our lives.

I once heard a story about a famous preacher who went to a nursing home to visit Alzheimer's patients. He went around and greeted people who were very glad to see him. He walked up to one lady and asked, "Do you know who I am?" She said, "No, but if you go to the front desk, they can tell you."

Is this your story? Have you been asking others who you are for so long that you have lost sight of your true self? Do you feel as if you have amnesia and that you are desperately trying to find out who you are? If any of this describes you, I know exactly how you feel. I remember a time in my life when I tried to be so many different people that I truly lost sight of what I enjoyed, what I wanted to do, and what I felt I should be doing. All I did know was that I was unhappy. In my effort to please people in order to get their acceptance, I had lost sight of myself.

As I close this chapter, let me remind you that you are a new creature in Christ, and you are His beloved—unique, treasured, valued, and desired by God Himself. Even when you were a sinner, He loved you enough to die in your place, taking all the punishment for your sins. And had you been the only person on earth, He would have done it just for you. The next time you meet someone and they ask you what you do (as people often do), you can tell them what your job is, but never forget that you are much more than what you do—you are God's beloved!

CHAPTER 10

No Parking at Any Time

The Lord said to Moses, Why do you cry to Me? Tell the people of Israel to go forward!

—Exodus 14:15

One day I was riding in a car and my attention was drawn to a sign on the street that said NO PARKING AT ANY TIME. Immediately, I thought, *We all need a sign like that to remind us not to park our lives at the point of our pain or disappointment and remain there.*

You are probably reading this book because something or someone has wounded you in the past, and I want to encourage you not to park your life, dreams, and goals at the place of your pain and just give up on life. Keep going forward. God created us to be people who are always moving forward. Being successful in anything isn't a one-time achievement, but rather a continual state of being.

> *Being successful in anything isn't a one-time achievement, but rather a continual state of being.*

The apostle Paul is a great example of someone who kept going forward no matter how difficult it was to do so. Paul was sent by God to share the good news of the Gospel of Jesus Christ, but he experienced a lot of opposition. When tragedy struck in the form of shipwreck, a snakebite, prison time, or being abandoned by those who were his associates and friends, and even when he experienced what he called a "thorn in the flesh," Paul was the epitome of never giving up. Had he parked at the point of his pain, we might be missing the two-thirds of the New Testament that God used him to write! If you park at the point of your pain, the rest of the world will miss out on what God wants to do through you.

Paul spoke of missing the mark of perfection in his daily walk with God, but he said that the one thing he did was let go of what was behind and continue pressing toward his goal (Philippians 3:12–13).

When failure or trouble comes, moving forward isn't always easy, but it is what God wants us to do. Job loss, divorce, sickness, injustice, the death of a loved one, uncertainty, and confusion can stop us in our tracks if we let them. But it's during these times that it is most important to keep moving forward, even if it feels like you're only progressing a few inches at a time. Those inches will eventually add up to a lot of progress. It is easy to quit and give up, but it takes a lot of courage to keep going forward in the midst of personal pain.

I recall a time when one of my children was in trouble, and it was a situation that could have been seriously life-altering. Naturally, I was very concerned and was really hurting emotionally and mentally. There were days when I didn't even want to get out of bed, but God urged me to just get up and keep putting one foot in front of the other. During that time, I was scheduled to teach at a conference, and in between the sessions, I went to my room and cried. But when the time came for the next session, I put one foot in front of the other, and as I stepped out, God helped me do what I needed to do. In the end, the situation had a very good conclusion. What could have been a disaster turned into a lesson in wisdom that helped my child to make better choices in the future.

History is full of people who overcame the overwhelming odds and setbacks life threw their way. Helen Keller lost her sight and hearing, but she accomplished great things in spite of her disabilities. Franklin Roosevelt's paralysis could have defeated him, but he pressed on and served in the nation's highest office as president. History is filled with stories of ordinary people who accomplished extraordinary things because they didn't park their life at the point of their pain.

I vividly remember my father telling me, "You will never amount to anything," but with God's help I overcame those words.

> *God is calling you forward; don't let anything hold you back.*

We all have the same opportunity to overcome obstacles. All it takes is a firm faith in God and a lot of determination. It comes down to what you're going to settle for in your life. God is calling you forward, so I encourage you not to let anything hold you back.

As God's daughter, you are a new creature. All of the old things have passed away and all things are made new (2 Corinthians 5:17). Accept that truth found in God's Word as your new normal and refuse to park at the point of your pain.

If you have studied the Bible, I am sure you have heard of Abraham. God entered into a covenant with him and did great things through him that we all still benefit from. But you may not know that God had previously asked Terah, Abraham's father, to leave Ur of the Chaldees and go to the land of Canaan. Although Terah started on his journey, he did not finish it, so God later asked Abraham to go instead (Genesis 11–12). Canaan was the land of promise that God wanted to give to His children, but He needed someone to work through.

When God called Terah to go to Canaan, he left as he was

instructed to do, but when he came to a town called Haran, he settled there. I have often wondered that if Terah had kept going instead of settling somewhere along the way, perhaps God would have made the covenant with him that He ultimately made with Abraham. We don't know for sure, but it certainly seems to me that it would have been a possibility. How many people does God call to do something great before He finds someone who will go all the way through with Him to victory?

Why did Terah settle or park somewhere along the way instead of going all the way through to the place God wanted him to go? Perhaps the way became difficult, or he may have gotten tired of traveling. I suppose we will never know, but I do know that the Bible says that Terah lived 205 years and died in Haran (Genesis 11:31–32). He died where he parked.

Terah settled for less than God's best in his life. Don't let that happen to you. God has always had a very good plan for you and your life (Jeremiah 29:11), and the things that have hurt you may have delayed it, but they cannot stop it as long as you won't stop. Don't stop moving forward!

Later, after Terah died, God called Abraham to make the journey, and he went all the way through with God and became the patriarch from whom all Jews trace their ancestry. God promised that He would make a great nation through him, and He did. Although Abraham's faith was tested, he passed his tests and was part of the ancestral lineage of Jesus Christ.

Perhaps you are facing a time of testing in your life right now and the temptation to quit and give up is strong. Know this: You have what it takes to go through it and experience victory because God is on your side!

> *You have what it takes to experience victory because God is on your side!*

We often try to leap over our problems or find a way to go around them so we don't have to deal with them, but that never produces good results in our life. We might avoid dealing with them for a long time, but they will remain in our way until we find the courage to go through them. If we hope to see the end fulfillment of our dreams, we need to go all the way through the things that are blocking our path. We cannot go part of the way and then park when life is difficult.

> But we do [strongly and earnestly] desire for each of you to show the same diligence and sincerity [all the way through] in realizing and enjoying the full assurance and development of [your] hope until the end (Hebrews 6:11).

The Lady in the Van

Shortly after God gave me the idea to encourage people not to park at the point of their pain, I saw a movie called *The Lady in the Van*, which had a big impact on me. The movie is based on a true story about Miss Shepherd, a homeless woman who lived in a yellow van parked in the driveway of Alan Bennett in London for fifteen years. Why? Because she had been hurt in her younger years, she was brokenhearted and had become disillusioned with life. She felt like a failure, and she experienced tremendous guilt during her life for accidentally killing a man while driving her van. All of these things caused her to give up on life. She parked her van and didn't move until her death.

Miss Shepherd was once a gifted and sought-after concert pianist. She felt that she wanted to serve God with her life, and the only way she knew to do that was to enter a convent and become a nun. The convent had a piano, and she enjoyed and was fulfilled in playing it in the evenings. However, the Mother Superior for some reason didn't like Miss Shepherd, or perhaps she was jealous of her talent, and she told her that she loved playing too much and that God was requiring her to sacrifice the piano to prove her love for Him. She obeyed, but it broke her heart. She was wounded in her soul, and the wounds caused her to withdraw from other people, as well as demonstrate other unique behaviors. She ultimately had to leave the convent and did so feeling rejected, abandoned, and alone.

The pain of these events ate at her mental and emotional health until she eventually was placed in a mental health facility. After being released from there, she ended up living in her old, worn-out van, which she painted yellow. After parking it various places and eventually being asked to move from each one of them, she talked Alan Bennett into letting her park in his driveway for what was supposed to be a short while, but she never left. And fifteen years later, she died where she parked.

In the movie, when she went to heaven, the first person she met was the man she thought she had killed, who immediately told her, "My death was not your fault; I purposely stepped out in front of your van to end my life."

I found myself thinking about this movie for days after I saw it, and I finally watched it a second time just to get the full impact of the message. For the movie producer, it may have just been a good story to tell, but for me it was a classic example of what we do in our own lives when our souls are deeply wounded. We park at the point of our pain, and we miss out on the best life that is available to us through Jesus Christ.

God's Promise of Healing and Restoration

We may not be able to avoid the pain we encounter in life that wounds our soul, but we can choose not to let it ruin the remainder of our life. Don't get stuck in a moment in time. No matter what happens to us, life goes on, and we can either go with it or stay behind, imprisoned in our pain and bitterness.

God promises to heal and restore us, but it does not happen magically with no action on our part. We believe the promises of God, and no matter how difficult it is to go forward, we keep going. Paul encourages us not to draw back and shrink in fear (Hebrews 10:38). Paul told the Hebrews, who were suffering greatly, that by faith in Jesus Christ they would preserve their souls. To preserve means to keep something safe.

> But our way is not that of those who draw back to eternal misery (perdition) and are utterly destroyed, but we are of those who believe [who cleave to and trust in and rely on God through Jesus Christ, the Messiah] *and* by faith preserve the soul (Hebrews 10:39).

Don't draw back, don't shrink in fear, don't get stuck in a moment of time, and don't park at the point of your pain. Every step of faith that you take is another step toward wholeness and healing.

The apostle Peter was used by God to heal a man who had been bedridden for eight years (Acts 9:33–34). He said to him, "Aeneas, Jesus Christ (the Messiah) [now] makes you whole." But he also said something else to him that we need to see. He said, "Get up and make your bed!" You see, this infirm man had been knocked down by life and had never gotten up. Peter told him it was time to get up. Jesus encountered a similar situation, except the man He encountered had been lying down for thirty-eight years, waiting for a miracle. He was waiting for someone to come along and fix his problem.

Jesus told him to get up, pick up his bed (sleeping pad), and walk (John 5:5–8). Jesus told him to do the impossible. He had been an invalid for a long time, and now he was being told to get up. Perhaps you feel like that invalid as you read this book. You might be thinking, *Joyce, you are asking me to do things that are just impossible. They are simply too hard!* But the truth is that all things are possible with God, and nothing that He asks us to do is too hard if we draw on His strength to enable us to do it.

Jesus is our Healer, but there will be things that He asks us to do on our journey, and if we don't do them, then we won't experience the healing He is making available. I wonder how many people may have encouraged Miss Shepherd to get out of the yellow van and improve her life, and yet she took no action. Somehow to her, the misery of the van was better than taking a chance on getting out of it and going forward.

It Is Not Too Late

I'm sure one of the lies the devil has told you is that it is too late for you. However, it is never too late for God to heal and restore anyone. The invalid had been in the condition he was in for thirty-eight years, and he got up and was made whole.

It is never too late to dust off your dreams and start moving forward. I'm sure that Miss Shepherd could have still played the piano beautifully if she had had the courage to try.

New beginnings and fresh starts are never in short supply with God. You may feel forgotten and worn-out, but God has not forgotten you. New and exciting things are waiting for you, all you need to do to get started in your new life is get up and keep on going. Here is God's promise for you. Hang on to it and don't look back!

> Do not [earnestly] remember the former things; neither consider the things of old.
> Behold, I am doing a *new* thing! (Isaiah 43:18–19; emphasis mine).

A woman we read about in the Bible named Ruth refused to park at the point of her pain or draw back to a miserable life. Her husband, brother-in-law, and father-in-law all died, and she was left with a decision to either press forward with her mother-in-law, who was very poor and had no way to provide for them, or to go back to her own country where she had previously worshipped idols.

Fresh starts are never in short supply with God.

She had come to believe in the one true God and obviously found life with Him to be better than where she came from, even if it meant some difficult times. Her mother-in-law urged her to go back, reminding her that she had no way to provide for her, but Ruth said that she would not go back. The two of them pressed forward, and Ruth eventually married a very wealthy man named Boaz. Ruth became the great-grandmother of David and is named as one of the five women in the genealogy of Jesus mentioned in Matthew chapter 1.

Little did Ruth know at the time that her decision would position her for greatness. But the outcome depended on her decision. A woman who had lost everything refused to believe it was too late for a new beginning! (For the full story of Ruth, see the Book of Ruth in the Bible.)

I believe you, too, are positioned for greatness. Make the right decision—the decision to press past your pain and enjoy all that God has planned for you.

CHAPTER 11

You Are Not Damaged Goods

*And in Him you have been made complete, and He is the
head over all rule and authority.*

—Colossians 2:10 NASB

I received Christ as a nine-year-old girl while visiting relatives
who took me to church with them. My life didn't seem to change
much as a result of me asking Jesus to forgive my sins and save
me, but I can recall lying in bed at night as a young adolescent
and teen, thinking, *Someday I am going to do something great!* I
now realize that was my new, born-again spirit talking. My heart
had changed, and whereas I was hopeless before, I now had hope
that the abuse I was experiencing would someday be over.

I had other thoughts that were not so positive. I can remember as a teenager intending to leave home as soon as I was out of
high school and reached the age of eighteen. I thought about my
life and what I might do or what might happen to me, and I vividly recall thinking, *I will always have a second-rate life because my
father abused me.* I saw myself as damaged goods, someone who
would always need to settle for whatever I could get in life. I actually planned on having a second-rate life, and that is sad.

I would like to say that the messages I heard from my born-
again spirit drowned out the negative and defeating messages
I received, but they didn't—at least not for several more years.

Occasionally, I had glimmers of hope, but the negativity in my mind always drowned it out. Per-haps you, too, bounce back and forth between believing things can be better for you and then doubting

> God will help you get to where you need to be.

that they ever will. Don't despair; God will meet you where you are and help you get to where you need to be.

I left home, and before long, I met a boy who was good-looking and paid attention to me. He asked me to marry him after we knew each other for a few months, and although I felt caution and a lack of peace in accepting his offer, I did it anyway. That deci-sion added more pain to my already crushed and wounded soul, and for five years he abused me in ways I had not experienced previously. He was unfaithful regularly. He didn't work most of the time and turned into a petty thief who stole from friends and relatives in order to go out and party with his friends.

One night I woke up realizing he was trying to get my wedding ring off of my finger. It wasn't worth that much, but I knew he intended to sell it. We had one child, and while I was pregnant, he lived with another woman, claiming that the baby I was car-rying was not his. I lived alone during my pregnancy and worked until I couldn't work any longer and found myself at a point of having no money or place to live. Thankfully, a woman I knew who cut and styled my hair was kind, and she offered to let me live with her and her mother until I had the baby.

After I gave birth to our son, my husband came to the hospital and wanted us to get back together, and as usual, I took him back. It was very common for him to abandon me for other women and eventually come back, telling me how sorry he was, and I always took him back. This type of behavior is common with women who have wounded souls. Because they see themselves as deserving nothing better, or they are afraid of being alone all their lives, they keep letting men abuse them in different ways rather than standing up for themselves.

When he and I left the hospital with our son, whom I had named David, we had no place to go. Although I had never slept on the street or in my car, I was without a home during that period of time and needed to depend on the kindness of others to help me. My husband had a former sister-in-law who was divorced from his brother. She was a kind, Christian woman, and she let us live in a room in her house until I went back to work and we could move. Very shortly after we moved, my husband once again left with another woman, and at that point, I just couldn't take it any longer and filed for divorce.

At that point in my life, I was buried under so many layers of emotional pain and fear about the future that I felt completely hopeless. I remember praying and asking God to someday just let me be happy and give me someone who truly loved me, and one year later He answered that prayer. I met Dave, whom I have been married to for over fifty years. The first twenty years of that marriage were very difficult.

My soul had been damaged. I didn't think, feel, or behave right. That is what happens to us when our souls are wounded. We see everything through the lens of our brokenness and pain, and it is difficult to believe that anything in life will ever get better. I had multiple fears, and yet I acted as if nothing frightened me. I lived with a fake boldness that actually manifested in me trying to control everyone around me so they couldn't hurt me. I thought I was being bold, but I was actually being rude and unkind.

I was insecure but tried to pretend that I wasn't. I was dishonest with myself and everyone else, and my life had become one of pretending in some area most of the time. Simply remembering how I once was reminds me of how great our God is! Truly He has delivered me from multiple problems and has healed my wounded soul.

Whole and Complete

When we put ourselves in God's healing hands, we may begin broken and damaged, but we end up whole and complete, without any evidence we were ever marred. When I talk about the way I used to be, I feel like I am talking about someone I once knew, who is now only a vague memory.

If we realize that we are made complete in Christ, then we never have to believe we are damaged and have to settle for second best in life. To be complete in Christ means that whatever we might be lacking, He makes up for it. His strength shows itself in our weakness (2 Corinthians 12:9); our sin is swallowed up by His mercy and forgiveness. Our past disappears in the light of the new life He offers us.

When we are born again, we receive God's Spirit and our spirit is made whole, complete, and totally new, but we still need work done in our soul. God does the work from the inside out, using His Word and our fellowship with Him to continue the work He has begun. Gradually, the complete and perfect thing that God by His grace did in our spirit is worked into our soul. When I say that we are complete and whole in Him, it is a true fact. That is who we are in Christ. It has taken place, yet we may not always think, feel, or behave as if we are whole—but we will if we keep moving forward in faith.

Here is an example that I think will help make my point clear.

Recently, I had a total hip replacement. In my doctor's words, the surgery is quite barbaric. Muscles are pulled and stretched to enable the surgery team to get to the hip joint, and when they do, they use a saw to remove the joint from the femur bone in the leg. The new joint is put in place and attached, the cut from the surgery is closed up, and the healing begins. Although I was able to get on my feet and walk while leaning on a walker the same day, healing has been gradual. I've consistently improved, but there were periods of a few days, or even an entire week, when I felt that I was making no progress at all. During those times, Dave reminded me to be patient. Now I am at the point where I have no real pain, but the muscles in the front of my leg are still sore. But after a little more time goes by, I won't even be able to tell that I ever had surgery.

Using that example, let's think about the emotional wounds we have from being abused or hurt in some way. When we are born again (receive Jesus as our Savior), He makes us complete and whole in our spirit, but we may continue for a period of time noticing things in our emotions, thinking patterns, and behavior that are not fully restored yet. One way to say it might be: "Jesus heals our wounds but sometimes the bruising lingers for a while." I came home with a new hip, but my entire hip and all the area around it was extremely bruised.

When it comes to the healing of our soul, it is very important during the process not to believe that nothing has changed in our life and go back to feeling like we are damaged beyond repair. When Jesus comes into your life, you are made brand-new inside, and that change is being worked from the inside to the outside, where everyone can see the amazing work God has done in you. Be patient.

If Only

Don't let the devil convince you that because you were abused or misused it means that your life could never be as good as it would have been if things had been different for you. Don't live with the thought, *If only*. None of your past has to matter if you don't let it matter. I've shared with you the tragic things I have gone through, and yet in my life today, there is no evidence I was ever damaged. When God makes something new, it is completely new!

Even after becoming a Christian, I wasted a lot of years with thoughts like this: *Things are better for me, but they would be really great if only I had not have been abused. I wouldn't have some of the problems I have now if only I had had a normal childhood with parents who really loved me properly.*

I attended a church for over ten years, and I learned some valuable things, but they taught me nothing about emotional healing or ever dealt with the trauma people experience after being abused. Once I started reading the Word and seeking God myself, I began to experience God's healing power, and I sometimes thought, *I would be a lot further along* if only *my previous church had taught me better.*

If we go down that path, we will never run out of things to say *if only* about. We cannot go back and change the way things were, but we can go forward and never look back. Instead of saying things would be good *if only* this or that were different, say, "I trust God to take what happened and work it all out for my good and make me a better person because of it."

> *We cannot change the way things were, but we can go forward and never look back.*

Where Is the Evidence?

You may have been wounded or damaged at one time, but the time will come when there will be no evidence in your life that it ever happened. I don't think anyone would look at my life now and see any evidence I was ever abused, abandoned, divorced, and almost homeless. Countless others can testify to the same thing in their own lives, and even if you are not there yet, you will be if you don't give up.

There is a story in the book of Daniel about three young men who chose to be put into a fiery furnace rather than bow down and worship anyone other than God. A decree had gone out that anyone who did not bow down to the king would suffer in the furnace, and they were expected to die there. Shadrach, Meshach, and Abednego refused to bow down, and into the furnace they went. Their actions so infuriated King Nebuchadnezzar that he ordered the furnace to be made seven times hotter than normal. It was so hot that the flames from it killed the men handling the furnace! The three young men were in the furnace in the midst of the flames, but when the king looked in, he amazingly saw four men and witnessed that the fire was not harming Shadrach, Meshach, and Abednego! We know the fourth Man in the furnace was the Angel of the Lord, a manifestation of Jesus.

When the king had the furnace opened and the three men came out, the Bible states that they were not harmed. Daniel 3:27 says, "The fire had no power upon their bodies, nor was the hair of their head singed; neither were their garments scorched or changed in color or condition, nor had even the smell of smoke clung to them."

You can come out of the fiery furnace of life, and there will be no evidence you were ever in it. Not even the smell of the life you once lived will cling to you. You are not damaged goods, and I urge you not to think that you are. Don't plan for a second-rate life, but instead plan on an amaz-ing life in which you do amazing things.

> *Plan on an amazing life in which you do amazing things.*

Eat Always at the King's Table

King Saul had a grandson named Mephibosheth. He was the son of Jonathan, who was in covenant relationship with David, who became king after Saul. Biblical covenant relationships were taken very seriously, and long after Saul and Jonathan had died, David was still searching for anyone of his bloodline that he might bless in order to honor his covenant with Jonathan.

> And David said, Is there still anyone left of the house of Saul to whom I may show kindness for Jonathan's sake? (2 Samuel 9:1).
>
> The king said, Is there not still someone of the house of Saul to whom I may show the [unfailing, unsought, unlimited] mercy *and* kindness of God? Ziba replied, Jonathan has yet a son who is lame in his feet (2 Samuel 9:3).

The boy lived in a town called Lo-debar, and that name meant "without pasture." It sounds like a dry and miserable place. Even while we are living in dry and miserable places, God is looking for us because He wants to bless someone for Jesus' sake. God doesn't bless us because we deserve it, but simply because He told Jesus that He would bless all those who believe in Him. Mephibosheth wasn't seeking a change in his life, but David was seeking him.

He was the grandson of the former king, yet he lived in miserable circumstances, although he could have been eating continually at the king's table because of the covenant relationship that existed between his father and King David.

When Mephibosheth was brought before David, he responded in fear. David told him not to be afraid, because he would show him kindness for his father's sake and restore all that was rightfully his. He also told him that he would always eat at his table.

Just think of it—God intends to restore everything that you have lost! He has sought you out and is inviting you to always eat at His table of blessing and joy.

The way Mephibosheth responded to David's offer tells us why he was living so far below his inherited right.

> And [the cripple] bowed himself and said, What is your servant, that you should look upon such a dead dog as I am? (2 Samuel 9:8).

Do you see it? He lived a second-rate life because he saw himself as damaged goods. He had an image of himself as a dead dog. Wow. That can teach us a huge lesson if we will let it. Have you been living an inferior life because you have a poor self-image? Do you feel worthless, damaged...as if it is too late for you? If so, it is time to move out of Lo-debar (a dry and miserable place) and into the King's castle!

From that day forward David provided everything that Mephibosheth and his young son Micha needed, and the Bible says he ate continually at the king's table even though he was lame in both feet (2 Samuel 9:13). I love that part. It helps me realize that even though we are lame (have weaknesses), we can still eat at our King Jesus' table.

Have you been crawling around under the table, being satisfied with the crumbs that fall on the floor? Have you settled for less than God's best? Imagine how you would feel if you prepared a wonderful meal and called your children to come and eat, and they all got under the table and began to tell you how worthless they were and that they were not qualified to sit at the table. That is how God feels when we refuse to receive His blessings because we believe we are damaged and therefore not worth anything. Jesus paid a high price for our healing and restoration when He died on the cross, so let's start receiving the benefits He purchased for us with His sacrifice.

You don't have to sacrifice anymore because Jesus has done it for you—now you can sit at the table and eat with the King!

CHAPTER 12

The Wounds of Sin

My wounds are loathsome and corrupt because of my fool-ishness.

—Psalm 38:5

Our souls are wounded from the terrible things that others do to us, but often we are also wounded from our own sin. Sometimes the deepest wounds in our soul are the result of personal sin and the effect it has had on our minds, emotions, and how we view ourselves in general. We may be riddled with guilty thoughts and feelings, and experience self-rejection or even self-hatred.

Our sins not only wound us, but they also wound the people we love and care about. Julie is a parent with adult children who are wounded, and she is the one who wounded them. She was an alcoholic and was either absent from the home or passed out and unavailable. There were also many times when she displayed violence during her drunken state. As a result of her alcoholism, she and her husband divorced. She eventually went to a treatment center, but by then her son was angry and acting out, and her daughter was depressed and withdrawn. What is Julie to do now? She is truly sorry for the pain she has caused them, and she has told them so, but everyone is left with wounds in their soul, including Julie.

Before her children were out of the home, Julie received Jesus and attended church regularly. She wanted them to attend with her, but they were in their late teenage years by then and had no interest. They went to college and eventually married and had children of their own, but their relationships with Julie remained distant. It was obvious they were full of resentment and preferred to spend as little time with their mother as they possibly could.

Now Julie has wounds in her soul from knowing that she hurt her children and wounds from feeling rejected by them. Although she does understand why they feel the way they do, it continues to be painful. What can she do? What can heal those types of wounds? I have some suggestions that are based in Scripture that will help:

The first thing to do is talk openly with God about your past, telling all and holding nothing back. King David sinned greatly by committing adultery with Bathsheba and having her husband, Uriah, murdered to prevent him from knowing what David had done. He then took her for his wife. David somehow managed to ignore his sin for almost one year, but it finally made him miserable enough that he had to confront it.

I would like to share with you in my own words what David said. *When I was silent, before I confessed my sin, I felt as if I were wasting away and my soul groaned all day long. I knew that You, God, were displeased, and I continually felt You dealing with me. My soul felt as if I were living in a drought in summer. I finally acknowledged my sin. I didn't hide anything, and I confessed until everything was out in the open. When I did, You instantly forgave my iniquity and guilt* (paraphrase of Psalm 32:3–5).

Although God already knows everything we do at all times, it is important for us to acknowledge our wrongdoing fully because that helps cleanse it from our souls. We can talk to God at any time about anything and know that we will never experience judgment or rejection. Talking about the things that are hidden in darkness is often the very thing that releases us from them. God desires truth in the inner being (Psalm 51:6).

Don't ever be so afraid of the light that you choose to remain in darkness. Although David had ignored his sin for a long time, it is obvious from his confession that he felt the weight of it. Perhaps he stayed so busy that he did not have to deal with it, or he may have made excuses for it—at least I know that is what I have often done in the past to avoid dealing with my own wrong behavior. Another way we may avoid dealing with our sin is to blame it on someone else. We may have ourselves convinced that if they wouldn't have done what they did, then we wouldn't have done what we did. Although there may be a grain of truth in that kind of thinking, we will never be free from the burden of sin unless we take responsibility for it and bring it out into the open—first with God and then, if necessary, with people.

> *Don't be so afraid of the light that you choose to live in darkness.*

The next thing to do is receive the forgiveness you have asked for. Receive it by faith and remember that your feelings may not change immediately. Learn and meditate on Scripture about the forgiveness of God and the amazing mercy of God until these truths become a revelation in your life. Once that happens, your feelings will line up with the truth of God's Word. Remember that once David acknowledged his sin with a repentant heart, God *instantly* forgave him. Jesus has already paid for our sins, and forgiveness is available if we will draw on it by faith.

Talk openly with the people you have wounded. You may need to go a little further than simply saying you are sorry. Share with them what you were going through at the time you hurt them and how deeply sorry you are for what you did. Humbly ask them to forgive you and give you another chance. Don't make excuses, because if you do, it will lessen the effect of your apology.

If they are either unwilling or unable to forgive you right away, tell them you understand and pray for them on a regular basis. Ask God to give them the grace to forgive you because He is truly the only One who can do that. Ask Him to heal the wounds in their souls.

Continue to show love toward them as opportunity presents itself. Love covers a multitude of sins (1 Peter 4:8). It also has the ability to melt even the hardest heart. When we continue to be kind and loving to those who are hardened against us, it will eventually have a wonderful healing effect on them.

You will need to be patient, because it will probably take time for the people we have hurt to believe we have changed and are truly sorry. We need to remember that just as our wounds have taken time to heal, theirs will also.

Don't Live with the Weight of Blame

Even if something that we did hurt someone, that doesn't mean that we must live eternally with feelings of guilt and blame. Once we have repented and asked others to forgive us for any pain that we have caused them, we need to let go of the blame. To blame means to accuse or condemn, so it is important for you to stop accusing yourself and blaming yourself for past mistakes. God's Word promises that there is no condemnation for those who are in Christ (Romans 8:1). Jesus did not come into the world to condemn it, but to save it (John 3:17).

My oldest son, David, was an angry young man and very rebellious for several years as a teenager and young adult. I recall a day when I was trying to correct his behavior and he said, "I wouldn't be this way if you would not have treated me the way you did." *Ouch!* I felt the sting of his words and walked away feeling condemned.

> *Jesus did not come into the world to condemn it, but to save it.*

What did he mean? Because of the abuse in my childhood, I was angry and very difficult to please, and David was on the receiving end of some of the anger and dysfunctional behavior in my life. I did a lot of yelling at my kids and pressured them to be what I wanted them to be instead of helping them be what God wanted them to be. By the time David was a young teenager, I was in a better place in my life, but he was still resentful about the past.

Although I had sincerely apologized to him, explaining that I was wrong and wanted things to be better between us, he frequently pulled the "It is your fault that I am this way" card. It was his way of blaming me rather than taking responsibility for his behavior. I clearly remember one day walking away from his room, feeling very guilty after he accused me of being the source of his bad behavior, but God began to speak clearly to my heart. He showed me that I had done all I could do and that carrying a burden of blame would never fix the situation. He told me my son had the same opportunity that I did to heal from the wounds of the past, and if he refused to do so, then I could do nothing else except entrust him to God.

That was very helpful to me, and I was able to release the situation to God. Interestingly enough, David never again told me that it was my fault he was angry and rebellious. Our relationship continued to grow, and now he is over fifty years old and tells me frequently how much he loves and respects me.

I believe it was important for me to stop carrying the blame in order for God to work in the situation. If you are carrying blame from something you have done in the past, I urge you to release it and realize that although you cannot go back and undo something you have done that hurt someone else, there is nothing that is impossible for God. He can change the heart of the one you hurt and heal the wounds you both have.

I admit that when we have deeply hurt someone, it is very difficult to release the burden of our actions, but it truly is the only thing we can do in order to go on with life.

I Want to—but It Is Too Hard

We should not park at the point of our pain that was caused by what others have done to us or what we have done to them. Doing so can leave us with wounded souls. But God offers us a new beginning, and that means we must put the past behind us and not look back. Let go of all blame, shame, and guilt from the past, and let God show Himself strong in your life.

Jesus said that no one putting his hand to the plow and looking back is fit for the kingdom of God (Luke 9:62). I believe that means that we cannot experience the amazing life God is offering unless we stop looking back at all of our mistakes from the past. Letting go of the past may be hard to do, but it is much better than reliving it every day of your life.

Be careful about thinking and saying that the things God asks you to do are too hard. God gives us His Spirit to do hard and difficult things, to do things that people who live without God in their lives are not able to do. Too frequently, I hear people say, "I know what God wants me to do, but it is just too hard." I also see them continue to live lives that are unhappy and unfulfilling.

Being convinced that doing God's will is too hard often causes people to backslide in their commitment to Christ. At one time they fully intended to obey the Lord, but when He asked them to do something that was difficult, they decided it was just too hard and went back to their old way of living. Many of the disciples who once followed Jesus turned back to their old way of life when He asked them to do things that they perceived as being too hard (see John 6:60–66). God never asks us to do anything unless He enables us to do it. He wants us to believe and take steps of faith, and when we do, we will discover that with God all things are possible!

Stop Punishing Yourself

We are invited into a relationship of trusting God for absolutely everything, and one of those things is trusting Him to take care of the past with all of our mistakes and the pain we experience from them.

No matter what you have done, and no matter how bad it was, there is a new beginning for you. Believing that is the first step toward your new life. When I initially tried to let go of the things I had done that hurt others, I felt guilty for even trying to let them go. I knew I was guilty, and I felt I should be punished. We frequently feel that we deserve punishment, so we punish ourselves by continuing to be miserable. But the good news of the Gospel of Christ is that He took our punishment. He was wounded for our transgressions (Isaiah 53:4–5). He actually carried the pains of the punishment that we deserve. Since He was punished for our sins, we no longer need to—nor should we—punish ourselves. If we continue to punish ourselves, then Christ died in vain. Stop and ask yourself if you are still punishing yourself for things you have done wrong in the past, and if your answer is yes, it is time to let it go.

How amazing would it be if someone were in prison for life for a crime they had committed and one day the jailer came to their cell, opened the door, and said, "You are free because someone has offered to serve your sentence and take your punishment." How foolish would they be to say, "No, I cannot let go of what I have done. I want to stay here and continue suffering. I want to be punished." Most of us can easily agree that would be foolish and that almost no one would do it, yet we do the same thing if we reject what Jesus has done for us.

Jesus became our substitute—He has suffered and has been punished for our sins. He was wounded for our transgressions. His wounds have healed our wounds, but that only becomes a reality in our life when we believe it and let go of the past.

You can trust God with all the mistakes of your past. He is able to heal and save to the uttermost (Hebrews 7:25). No one is beyond His reach—not you, and not the people you may have hurt.

CHAPTER 13

Learning to Live Inside Out

I have been crucified with Christ. It is no longer I who live, but Christ who lives in me. And the life I now live in the flesh I live by faith in the Son of God, who loved me and gave himself for me.

—Galatians 2:20 ESV

When we accept Christ as our Savior, He does an amazing work in us. He comes to live inside of us and gives us a new nature and a new spirit, both of which are His. Everything that Jesus is comes to live inside of us, in our born-again spirit.

We receive His righteousness, His peace, His joy, and the fruit of His Spirit. We are justified in Him, redeemed in Him, and sanctified in Him. We have the mind of Christ, we are forgiven, we are dead to sin—and this is only the beginning of what God's Word says that we are and have in Christ.

Have you ever been so discouraged with the way your life has turned out that you thought or said, "I wish I had someone else's life"? That is exactly what you get when you receive Jesus as your Savior—He takes your old life and you get His life. In Galatians 2:20, Paul said that he had been crucified with Christ and that he no longer lived, but Christ lived in him and the life he was living now, he lived by faith.

Paul was living a new life, one in which he had learned to put his trust in Jesus for everything rather than putting it in himself or other people. He exchanged his old life for a new life lived in Christ. Here is a partial list of the things God's Word says are ours in Christ. This is literally what we get when we receive Jesus...

- We are complete in Him, who is the Head of all principality and power (Colossians 2:10).
- We are alive with Christ (Ephesians 2:5).
- We are free from the law of sin and death (Romans 8:2).
- We are far from oppression, and do not fear, for terror does not come near us (Isaiah 54:14).
- We are born of God, and the evil one does not touch us (1 John 5:18).
- We are holy and without blame before Him in love (Ephesians 1:4; 1 Peter 1:16).
- We have the mind of Christ (1 Corinthians 2:16; Philippians 2:5).
- We have the peace of God that passes all understanding (Philippians 4:7).
- We have the Greater One living in us; greater is He who is in us than he who is in the world (1 John 4:4).
- We have received the gift of righteousness and reign as kings in life by Jesus Christ (Romans 5:17).
- And so much more! (Find even more declarations in appendix II.)

All of the amazing things that become ours in Christ are quite astounding. We begin our walk with God by believing His promises are true, and only then will we begin to experience the reality of them in our daily lives. Most of the time people say, "I'll believe that when I see it," but God's promises must be believed first. Believe in your heart first and see later. Faith and patience are the keys that unlock the vault to God's promises (Hebrews 6:12).

Faith and patience are the keys that unlock the vault to God's promises.

Learning who we are in Christ is vital if we are to ever live a victorious life as a Christian. We are to believe we are dead to our past and let it go, while holding on to Jesus as we go forward. Our past may make a difference to some of the people we know, but it makes no difference at all to God. He sees us as a new person who has not only died with Christ but was also raised to a new life. Our goal should be to learn to see ourselves as God sees us. When we receive Christ, He takes our sin and gives us His righteousness. God views us as righteous. That is the way He chooses to see us once we are in Christ (2 Corinthians 5:21).

When we receive Jesus, not only does He come to live in us, but we are also placed in Him. He is in us, and we are in Him; we are made one and have union with Him. Paul said we are to be strengthened through our union with Him (Ephesians 6:10).

If we are in Him, then everything that He is becomes ours. We go to Him empty, and He fills us. If I am an empty jar and I am placed in a barrel of water, I will be filled with the water just as the barrel is. What is in the barrel becomes mine. When we are placed into Christ by virtue of our faith in Him, He fills us with Himself.

Countless Scripture verses speak of us being in Christ. One of them is found in Philippians 3:3, which says that our confidence is to be *in Christ* and not in our own ability to perform. We learn to find our worth and value in Him instead of in our own works or what we can do. Confidence is important, and I dedicate an entire chapter to it later in the book, but let me encourage you to never put your confidence in things that are shaky. Jesus is the Rock that we can depend on, and He is completely dependable.

The Deposit

If someone went to your bank and deposited several million dollars in your account, you would be able to draw on it for the rest of your life. Just imagine how awesome that would be. You would be grateful, happy, and excited and certainly would not continue barely getting by in life when so much was available to you.

Jesus has made a deposit in each of His children. According to Scripture, He has given us *all things* that pertain to life and godliness.

> For His divine power has bestowed upon us all things that
> [are requisite and suited] to life and godliness, through
> the [full, personal] knowledge of Him Who called us by
> *and* to His own glory and excellence (virtue) (2 Peter 1:3).

Please notice that "all things" are not experienced by us—even though in reality they belong to us—unless we are personally knowledgeable of Him and the kind of life He has called us to live. We have to add our diligence to the promises and exercise our faith in them in order to see them released into our lives.

If someone made the deposit in your bank account I mentioned above, but you didn't know it was there, then obviously you would never make a withdrawal. Lack of knowledge is the thing that prevents God's children from living the truly awesome life that Jesus died for them to have. They simply don't know that it is even an option. They have no idea they can let go of the past and never look back or that they can experience healing from all the wounds in their soul.

Likewise, if the deposit was made but the person was lazy and never went to the bank to get what they needed, they would also live in lack even though they actually were supplied with everything they could ever need.

Jesus has made a deposit in you of anything and everything you could ever need by making you His home and becoming your home. Everything we need and desire is in Him; He is in us and we are in Him. Please don't miss the benefit this truth is intended to give you because of lack of knowledge or being passive about claiming these promises as your own. Although I have known these things for over forty years, I am still astonished by the fact that God has chosen to live in us and has allowed us to live in Him. What an amazing privilege! If you can believe it, you can have it!

> On that day you will realize that I am in my Father, and
> you are in me, and I am in you (John 14:20 NIV).

Paul told the believers to stop boasting about the leader they were following and realize all things were theirs (1 Corinthians 3:21). In other words, we do not get what we need or find our worth and value from the people we attach ourselves to, but only from being in Christ and Him being in us.

I am sure this sounds good to you, but in order for it to become revelation (a reality) to you, I recommend that you meditate on it daily. Think and say, "I am in Christ, and He is in me. I am His home, and He is my home." Remind yourself of it daily so you never lose sight of it. After over forty years of studying God's Word, I still remind myself of these amazing promises several times each week.

Close Fellowship with Jesus

We are invited to have close fellowship with Jesus through His Spirit. He told His disciples that when He went away, He would send them another Comforter to be in close fellowship with them, and that is also His promise to us (John 16:7). You don't ever need to feel that Jesus is far away because He is as close to you as your breath or heartbeat. He is in you. You can talk to Him anytime. He wants to have a close, personal relationship with you.

Our ministry recently hosted an event, and I had an opportunity to speak personally with several people. I remember a woman and her husband who both cried as they tried to express to me how much the Word of God, which I have had the privilege of sharing, has done for them. I asked them to be specific, and they both said, "We only had religion, and we tried so hard to follow all the rules and regulations, and yet we always felt like a failure. But you taught us who we are in Christ and that we don't need to go searching for Jesus because He lives in us." I was so touched by their tears and the sincerity of their testimony.

They were actually expressing that they had learned how to live inside out, which is what this chapter is all about. Instead of trying to follow all the rules and regulations so they would feel that they had some value, they had learned that they were given value by the fact that Jesus died for them and had made them His home. They were now drawing daily on the deposit He has made in them, and as a result, they were amply supplied with everything they needed. They had confidence, security, strength, righteousness, peace, joy, and on and on the list goes. They knew that whatever need might arise, it was already met in Jesus, so they had no reason to live in fear. This is also your inheritance and mine and that of every other person who believes in Jesus.

As the home of God, He has formed and fashioned you very carefully and intricately. In Exodus, we can read about the guidelines that God gave Moses for constructing and erecting the tabernacle. There are three entire chapters of very precise details that include instructions for every pillar and socket and even the rings that held the curtains on the poles. There is specific instruction for construction of the mercy seat, the frame of the tabernacle, the type of materials that were to be used for the altar and every other item, the gold and silver overlays, the precious stones to be used, the embroidery, the exact measurements of each item, and other details. It is a very extensive and detailed list.

When I was reading Exodus and got to those chapters, I found it to be a little taxing on my mind to keep reading one detail after another for three entire chapters. Because I am very practical in my approach to God's Word, and I believe there is a practical message for us in each thing we read and study, I asked God, "What can I take away from this and use in my daily life?" Immediately, I felt that God showed me that since He was so precise in His instructions about the building of the tabernacle, I should ponder just how detailed and precise He surely was in creating and forming each of His children. He has fashioned each of us as a suitable home in which He can dwell. He took great care in forming us and was precise about each detail of our temperament, talents and abilities, the color of our hair and eyes, the skin tone we have, how tall we are, and every other detail of our creation. The good news is that we are not a mistake.

Because my voice is quite deep in tone for a woman, I did not like it at all. I jokingly said, "I must have been in the wrong line when God handed out voices." But of course, that is not true, and you were not in the wrong line, either. Even if there are things about the way you are put together that you do not like, God does, and I recommend that you make peace with all the aspects of the way you are created. Instead of making yourself miserable by wishing for what you don't have, make a decision to accept yourself and do the best you can with what you have.

Psalm 139 is a wonderful chapter in the Bible that shares how carefully God formed us. He personally formed you with His own hand in your mother's womb, and you are fearfully and wonderfully made. Please read and study Psalm 139 slowly. Contemplate all it is saying and thank God for creating you. You are not a mistake; you are God's amazing design!

> *You are not a mistake; you are God's amazing design!*

Bearing Good Fruit

Jesus is the vine and we are the branches that are rooted in Him. We are expected to bear good fruit, to live righteously, walk in love with other people, be kind, and be humble. We are to be peaceful, joyful, and patient. And we are to use the abilities that God has given us to serve Him and help people.

God would never require us to produce anything if we had no ability to do so. That would be terribly frustrating to feel we had to do something and yet be left without the things we needed to do it. God makes a deposit in us of all the things He expects us to produce in our lives. He puts it in, and we let it come out. For example, He first loves us, so we have the ability to love others (1 John 4:19). Jesus left us His peace (John 14:27) so we could be peaceful in every situation that we encounter in life.

If we live, dwell, and remain in Him, and let His Word (Jesus) live, dwell, and remain in us, God's Word promises us that we will bear much good fruit (John 15:5). When we become Christians, we don't begin a journey of behavior modification, but one of learning to do life with Jesus. To live, dwell, and remain in Him simply means to fellowship with Him, lean on Him, trust in Him, rely on Him, learn His Word, and talk to Him about everything all the time. He is our source of all good things, and that certainly includes good behavior on our part. Learn to live inside out and your behavior will become more and more like Jesus'. Focus more on who you are in Christ, rather than struggling to modify your behavior.

Of course, we all want and need to see changes in ourselves. We are flawed as humans, and the world has taught most of us some very bad habits. We are learning a new way to live, and change is something we should all desire. But learning the right way to change, or be changed, is very important; otherwise, we will spend our lives frustrated and feeling like a failure.

We can modify our behavior somewhat through discipline and self-control, but we cannot change our nature—only God can do that, and He has. Our part is to believe it and learn to draw on what He has put in us instead of merely "trying" to be a "good Christian." Trust God to change the things in you that need to change. Keep pressing toward the mark of perfection as the apostle Paul did. And above all else, trust God's grace to work in you continually, enabling you to be all that He wants you to be. Because apart from Him, you can do nothing (John 15:5).

Everything you or I will ever need is in us—in Christ. We are strong *in Him*, and we can do all things *through Him*, who strengthens us (Philippians 4:13).

CHAPTER 14

You've Got What It Takes

I can do all things [which He has called me to do] through Him who strengthens and empowers me [to fulfill His purpose—I am self-sufficient in Christ's sufficiency; I am ready for anything and equal to anything through Him who infuses me with inner strength and confident peace].

—Philippians 4:13 AMP

Because God lives in us, we truly can do anything we need to do, but we are often defeated by our own wrong thinking. God says we can, but if we think and say that we can't, then we won't. This chapter is designed to remind you of how powerful you are *in Christ*. Don't ever forget that what you believe will become your reality. No matter how many wonderful things Jesus has done for us or deposited in us, they won't help us unless we firmly believe they are ours. Let's always remember that the devil is a liar, and if we believe his lies, then we become deceived just as Eve did in the beginning of time. Learning to believe and trust in God's Word more than we believe what we think or feel makes the difference in living victoriously or being defeated.

Like most of you, I regularly come up against things that are challenging and my first thought is often, *I can't do this.* But my second thought is, *I can do whatever I need to do through Christ.* That does not mean that everything I need to do is made easy by believing I can do it, but it does make it possible. We are instructed in God's Word to not faint in our minds (Hebrews 12:3). We shouldn't think that we are not capable of doing what God directs us to do. Our thoughts turn into our behaviors, so if we think we cannot do a thing, we are weakened to the point where we can't.

You are stronger than you may think you are. You can do whatever you need to do in life *through Christ,* and God's Word says that you are more than a conqueror through Him, who loves you (Romans 8:37). Notice it is "through Him," not through your own determination. We need to be determined and refuse to give up, but the greatest amount of determination will eventually dissipate unless we continually draw on God's strength that is in us.

What does it mean to be "more than a conqueror"? I believe it means that we can live life with confidence that we will win every battle we face even before it begins. We don't have to wait to see how big the problem is before we decide how things will turn out. Many things are impossible with us, but *nothing* is impossible with God!

When I am really tired because I've had a virus that I'm finally recovering from, and I am looking at a heavy travel schedule and several meetings that are not going to be very exciting, I am no different than anyone else—I am tempted to think and say, "I just can't do this." However, as I apply these principles I am sharing with you to my own life, they work every time. I end up being able to do everything I need to do—through Christ. I may not be excited about each part of it, but I do it—I conquer it!

If God is for us, who [can be] against us? [Who can be our foe, if God is on our side?]

Yet amid all these things we are more than conquerors *and* gain a surpassing victory through Him Who loved us (Romans 8:31, 37).

You Are Not Weak—You Are Strong!

The devil delights in making us think we are weak and incapable, but the truth is that we have all of God's strength available to us. We may be weak in ourselves, but His strength shows itself most effective through our weakness when we lean on and rely on Him.

Paul was dealing with a huge problem in his life that he referred to as "a thorn in the flesh" (2 Corinthians 12:7). We all have those from time to time: a person or a thing that just won't go away and is either painful or extremely challenging, or both. Paul begged God to let it depart from him, but instead, God told him that He would give him the strength to bear it.

> Three times I called upon the Lord *and* besought [Him] about this *and* begged that it might depart from me;
> But He said to me, My grace (My favor and loving-kindness and mercy) is enough for you [sufficient against any danger and enables you to bear the trouble manfully]; for *My* strength *and* power are made perfect (fulfilled and completed) and *show themselves most effective* in [your] weakness (2 Corinthians 12:8–9).

If God simply removed every difficulty from our lives, there would be no need for Him in our daily lives. He leaves a certain amount of weakness in each of us in order to have a place to show

Himself strong. He wants to be needed. He wants to be sought after. He wants us to believe that we can do whatever we need to do through Him.

Although my mother believed in God, she did not know how to rely on Him to be her strength. She did not confront the situation with my father in our home, and she allowed the incest to continue because she thought she was incapable of caring for my brother and me without him. She was not a strong woman because she saw herself as weak and incapable. If you see yourself as weak, you will allow people to mistreat you and you will always take a backseat in life. We cannot live the wonderful life that Jesus died to give us unless we believe that we are strong in Him.

Those of us who need healing for a wounded soul or recovery from tragic things that have happened to us need to believe that we are strong, not weak. There will be many times during your journey of healing that you will be tempted to think that you just do not have the strength to confront the issues that will need to be confronted, and you are right. On your own, you are too weak and not strong enough to do it, but God isn't weak. He is strong. Drawing on His strength will get you through anything if you don't falter, or faint, in your mind and give up. My mother could have had a good life herself, as well as my brother and me, if she could have believed this very important truth.

The psalmist David said, "My soul is weary with sorrow; strengthen me according to your word" (Psalm 119:28 NIV). Isaiah said, "He gives strength to the weary and increases the power of the weak" (Isaiah 40:29 NIV), and "Those who hope in the LORD will renew their strength. They will soar on wings like eagles;

they will run and not grow weary, they will walk and not be faint" (Isaiah 40:31 NIV).

Paul said, "Be strong in the Lord and in the power of His might" (Ephesians 6:10 NKJV). Psalms contains countless Scriptures that repeatedly say, "God is my strength." One of my favorites is, "But you, LORD, do not be far from me. You are my strength; come quickly to help me" (Psalm 22:19 NIV).

When we feel weak—and we all do at times—we should go immediately to Scripture and draw strength from God's Word. It is even better if we have studied the Bible long enough to have memorized verses that will help us at any time, without us even needing to get a Bible and look up verses. If we put the Word in us, the Holy Spirit will draw it out at the exact time we need it. He brings it to our remembrance (John 14:26).

Are you dealing with anything right now in your life that feels overwhelming to you? Have you been thinking that you just cannot do it or that the situation is simply too much for you? If so, let these Scripture verses teach you how to think the way God wants you to think. Believe that with Christ, you can do whatever you need to do in life.

We can do battle because the Word of God is a weapon. Every weak, incapable, I-can't-do-it thought that comes to us can be cast down by meditating on and confessing God's Word. I encourage you to form a habit of meditating on God's Word. To meditate means to think or ponder, contemplate, murmur, or speak God's Word.

Greater Is He That Is in You

We are indeed weak and incapable in many ways, but God, who is the greater One, lives in us. You've got what it takes to do what you need to do! You don't need to have fear in any situation. You may not know what is going to happen, how difficult things may become, how long it may be before victory is yours, or what to do—but God does, and He is living in you! He will guide you each step of the way if you continue to put your faith in Him. Let us learn to be "God inside minded." Remind yourself daily that God lives in you. He is close to you at all times and is always ready to help you.

Think about the promises in God's Word concerning who you are in Him and what you can do through Him until it becomes part of who you are. Don't just merely go to church once a week and perhaps read a daily devotional that requires five minutes or less and think that is enough to help you live as more than a conqueror. We should learn to identify with Christ at all times. We died with Him, and we are raised with Him to a new, powerful, and overcoming life. We are God's home, and He is our home. You have what you need to do whatever you need to do!

I am not a fan of weakness. I am sure that is partially because I experienced firsthand what my mother's weak mentality did to her, my brother, and me. But it is also because I know what my life would have turned out to be had I not learned to believe that greater is He that is in me than he who is in the world (1 John 4:4). I am asking you to really think about what you think of yourself and how you feel about your capa-

> *What you believe about yourself is more important than what anyone else believes.*

bilities. What you believe about yourself is much more important than what anyone else believes. Learn to believe what God says about you and what you can and cannot do.

This anonymous story from PassItOn.com really speaks to me:

A few years back when I was about ten, my grandfather was on his deathbed, and we were getting ready to leave the hospital—not knowing that it was the last time we would ever see him. Going around the room we all (yes the entire extended family was shoved into the little window side half of the room) went and gave him a hug goodbye. As my turn came up, I leaned over to hug him, and as I did he whispered in my ear, "You're gonna be a great man." Scared of what might happen to him, I started crying as we left the hospital, and yet began thinking of what he had said.

Those words have inspired me to this day, urging me to try my hardest and be the great man that my grandfather knew I could be. He has given me the strength and courage to be the best I can and to look to people that can help make that happen. I look forward to one day fulfilling his hope by working somewhere in the healthcare profession, helping others, as he helped me. Thanks Grandpa.

If this person could be this affected in a positive way by what his grandpa said, how much more can we be affected by what God says? When I was a young girl of nine or ten, I recall lying in bed thinking, *Someday I'm going to do something great!* There was no reason for me to think that, considering what was taking place in my life at the time, but I realize now that those thoughts began to slip into my mind only after I received Christ as Savior at the age of nine. When Jesus comes in, weakness goes out.

Those thoughts I had of doing great things were fleeting. They went out of my mind as quickly as they came in. At that young age I don't know what I thought about the possibility of ever overcoming my painful situation. I was merely trying to survive at that time. However, once I began studying God's Word and I put my confidence in Him and His promises, I remembered that thought I had had as a young girl. Without God, the things I am doing today would have never become a reality, but with Him all things are possible—not only for me, but for you, too. Will you make a decision today to believe it?

Whether you have a special needs child, are a single parent, are caring for elderly parents who are difficult to deal with, or have lost your job along with the retirement fund you paid into for twenty years, I want to promise you that you are not alone, and you can do what you need to do. You are stronger than you think you are!

If you were abused in unspeakable ways and your soul is filled with wounds that feel like open, bleeding sores—you are more than a conqueror through Christ, who loves you. You may not feel that way right now, but if you begin by believing it, eventually your feelings will catch up with your belief. I encourage you not to spend one more day feeling helpless, weak, and incapable. See yourself as a special, well-equipped child of God who has what it takes to do whatever needs to be done.

You Are More than a Survivor

We often hear people say that they are victims of abuse, or that they are survivors of abuse, but you are much more than that. You are an overcomer!

> Who is the one who overcomes the world, but he who believes that Jesus is the Son of God? (1 John 5:5 NASB).

I believe that as long as we see ourselves as victims, we continue to feel victimized and often carry resentment about our past. However, in Christ, our past does not need to determine our future.

Likewise, I believe that if we see ourselves as mere survivors, it still leaves us with thoughts of being someone who has barely come through a tragedy instead of someone who is strong and an overcomer. I never refer to myself as a victim of incest or a survivor of it. I am a new creature in Christ, and so are you if you believe in Jesus.

How we see ourselves and what we believe are extremely important. A story is told about a young man who had lost his job and all of his money. He was sitting on a park bench feeling very depressed and hopeless when an elderly gentleman noticed and asked why he was so sad. The man told his story, and at once the older gentleman took out a checkbook, wrote him a check, and said, "I will visit you at this same spot one year from today, and by then you will have made enough money to pay me back." When he looked at the check, he saw it was written for half a million dollars and signed John Rockefeller, who was at that time one of the wealthiest men in the world.

The man in the park put the check in his safe, and although he didn't cash it, it gave him confidence to believe that he didn't need to be afraid to start over. He began doing business again and started making money, always being aware that he had the check in the safe if he needed it.

The year went by, and by then he had plenty of money and was eager to return the check to the man who had helped him. He went back to the same park, sat on the same bench, and waited. Soon he saw the elderly gentleman approaching, but he had what appeared to be a nurse with him. The man seemed to be fairly unresponsive to the younger man, who was holding out the original check, trying to give it to him. The nurse took the check, looked at it, and said, "Oh, this is no good. He is confused most of the time. He often thinks he is Rockefeller, but he isn't."

The young man succeeded because he believed that he had what he needed in the bank and could draw on it at any time. What he had wasn't even a reality, but thinking that it was helped him overcome his loss.

What we have is so much more. We have something in the bank, so to speak, because we have Jesus living inside of us, and we can live without fear and do great things because we can make withdrawals anytime we need anything. If you need help, you can make a withdrawal. If you need peace, you can make a withdrawal. If you need wisdom, or strength, or creativity, make a withdrawal. You can never make too many withdrawals, because what you have available in Jesus has no limits. He is always more than enough for any need we have.

I want to say this as I close this chapter: You can do whatever you need to do through Christ, who is your strength. You are not weak; you are strong. You are more than a conqueror through Jesus. You are an overcomer!

CHAPTER 15

Roadblocks to Healing

And it will be said: "Build up, build up, prepare the road!
Remove the obstacles out of the way of my people."

—Isaiah 57:14 NIV

When we are wounded, we must not only desire to be healed, but we must be willing and ready to be brutally honest with ourselves. The truth makes us free (John 8:32), but facing truth is not always easy. We develop many ways to hide from truth, and they become roadblocks and hindrances to our healing.

I was not the cause of my wounds, and I wanted to be healed, but I eventually had to realize that even though I desired healing, I was not dealing with the roadblocks that needed to be removed.

When Jesus encountered a man who was in deep need of healing from wounds that he had carried for thirty-eight years, He asked him if he was serious about getting well (John 5:6). That seems like an odd question that is lacking compassion, but it isn't. No real effort is required in desiring a thing, but acquiring what one desires often requires overcoming a great many obstacles that are in the path of victory. Nothing worth having is ever acquired easily without effort or determination; therefore, if you are a wounded soul who desires healing, I need to ask you if you really want to get well.

I pray that you said yes and that you meant it, because however long or painful your journey of healing may be, the joy of eventually being free is well worth it. At some point, any person with a wounded soul must choose between remaining devastated and being healed and made completely whole.

Just because someone threw you in a pit of misery does not mean that you must remain there the rest of your life. God is ready to help. Are you ready to be made well?

> He drew me up out of a horrible pit [a pit of tumult and of destruction], out of the miry clay (froth and slime), and set my feet upon a rock, steadying my steps *and* establishing my goings (Psalm 40:2).

God gives us His promise of helping us, but we are partners with God in our healing, and we will need to do our part. God does not always magically deliver us from the things that stand in our way, but He always gives us the ability and power to confront them if we are willing to do so.

The Roadblock of Avoidance

The first roadblock we will need to deal with is the roadblock of avoidance, which is running away from or ignoring reality, hoping that if we ignore our problems long enough, they will go away. When I left home at the age of eighteen, I thought I had left all my problems behind me. After all, my father couldn't abuse me any longer because I wasn't living in his house, right? Actually, that isn't right. While it was true that he could no longer sexually or emotionally abuse me, the effects of what he had done would continue to torment me as long as I kept my pain buried and refused to deal with the effects of what I had been through. You may have heard the statement that it is our secrets that make us sick, and that was definitely true in my life. I left home and quickly married the first young man who showed any interest in me out of fear that I would never be loved by anyone else. But that relationship turned into five more years of emotional abuse.

After divorcing him, I met and married Dave Meyer, and he truly did love me, but I was so wounded that I deflected any effort he made to show me his love. I was suspicious of men in general, rebellious toward any kind of male authority, and insecure, which left me craving a constant outward show from others that I was acceptable and valuable. When people didn't make me feel the way I thought they should, I became angry and conveniently put the blame on whoever wasn't giving me what I wanted. And that is barely the beginning of the problems I had in my personality that hindered me from having meaningful, loving relationships. I had secrets buried deep in my soul, and it couldn't heal because I avoided dealing with the problems. Ignoring a problem never makes it go away.

> *Ignoring a problem never makes it go away.*

I thought that when I got away from my problems, like getting out of my father's house or divorcing my first husband, I could push down the memories of what had happened and just go on with life, but pain that we bury alive never dies. It just keeps hurting us until we let God help us dig it up and deal with it. After approximately five years of being married to Dave, we went to a seminar at our church where the teacher shared her testimony about her father sexually abusing her. Had I known that was to be the topic, I doubt I would have attended. But I didn't know, so there I was, hearing things that brought my own pain to the surface.

By that time, I had shared with Dave that my father had sexually abused me, but I had not shared in a way that would help me heal. I shared my past more as a way of excusing my current behavior than anything else. My attitude was: *I can't help the way I behave because I was abused.* Dave wanted me to get the help I needed, so he bought me a book the woman had written. The next day I opened it, and after reading two or three pages, I threw it across the room and said out loud (since no one was home but me), "I will not read this!"

Just reading some of the intimate details of what her father had done to her brought to the surface feelings and pain that I had buried and tried to forget, but obviously, they were still very much alive in my soul. Any time anything happened that caused them to even begin to surface, I pushed them down once again and tried to go on with life while ignoring the roadblocks that needed to be removed in order for me to live a life I could enjoy. Time and time again, I successfully avoided dealing with the root of my problems, but they always resurfaced, and I continued to be miserable.

This Time Was Different

I realized fairly quickly that this time was different, and trying to ignore the past wasn't going to work any longer. I had asked God to get involved in my life and help me be the person He wanted me to be. However, I didn't realize that would require me facing the past instead of continuing to run and hide from it. I heard two words gently but firmly spoken in my spirit. God simply said,

"It's time." I didn't need Him to explain what He meant because I instantly knew He was telling me that I had to face the past in order to go forward. It was time to remove the first roadblock.

We run from our problems in many different ways. When Jonah didn't want to do what God was asking him to do, he literally ran in the opposite direction from where he had been told to go. Jonah found himself in some very difficult and uncomfortable circumstances until he eventually followed God's direction (Jonah 1–3). Had I chosen to ignore the two words that God spoke in my heart at that time, I would still be in a pit of despair with all of my misery. Thankfully, I decided to follow God instead of my feelings, and my journey of healing began.

If you have been running from your past and you desire healing in your soul, let me say to you what God said to me: It's time! It is time to learn how to communicate with yourself honestly and stop blaming your past for any current problems that you have. Our past certainly may be the reason we behave in undesirable ways, but we should not let it become an excuse to stay the way we are. Buried feelings have energies of their own. They are alive, and they constantly affect us in adverse ways until we confront and deal with them. No matter how far down we have pushed them into our soul, they will manifest themselves in some way sooner or later. They will not ever simply vanish. They must be dealt with.

> You should not let your past become an excuse to stay the way you are.

Facing Reality

A wounded person may waste years of their life, and some even waste their entire life, trying to get something from someone that they simply don't know how to give. I wanted to have parents who truly loved me, but I had to face the reality that they had problems of their own and simply didn't know how to love me. One day I looked at myself in a full-length mirror and said, "My parents will never love me the way I want them to." I recall experiencing a degree of freedom as I walked away from the mirror. Simply facing that reality and deciding I was no longer going to set myself up for disappointment by wishing my parents were normal, loving parents brought relief to my soul. One would think that facing that fact would hurt, but it actually helped. Nothing is more frustrating than trying to get something from someone that they don't have and never will give us.

It was time for me to believe God's promise that even though my father and my mother had forsaken me, He would adopt me as His own child (Psalm 27:10). Even though God may not give you the thing you desire, He will give you something even better if you trust Him. God could not make my parents love me because He gives each of us free will, but if I was willing to face the truth about them and the pain they had caused and not be bitter because of it, then He would give me His love and acceptance. He would be my Father and my Mother and Sister and Brother and Friend and everything else I would ever need. And He wants to do the same thing for you.

Facing the past does not mean that we are to focus on it excessively, because that can be very destructive. God wants us to face it and move on. As God brings things up in your heart and lets you know that it is time to deal with something, don't put it off any longer. Pray about it, forgive anyone you need to forgive, and then let it go and move beyond it. It may be a decision you will have to renew frequently, but each time you do, you will experience a little more freedom from the pain of your past.

Thankfully, our Lord doesn't overwhelm us by showing us everything we need to deal with all at one time. He is an amazing Counselor who is kind and merciful, and He always gives us the grace (strength and ability) to do whatever He asks us to do.

Facing truth is painful, and for that reason many of us avoid it, but not facing it is even more painful. I often say there are two kinds of pain we can choose between: the pain of going forward or the pain of remaining where we are. Even though facing truth and going forward is painful, at least it is a type of pain that allows us to make progress, and that is far better than ongoing pain that will never end.

> There are two kinds of pain: the pain of going forward or the pain of remaining where we are.

As difficult as it is to face truth concerning what others have done to us, it is often even more difficult to face truth about what we have done that is wrong. This is especially true in some cases. For example, it is one thing to face the fact that the person you were married to was unfaithful and rejected you, but it might be even more difficult if the truth is that you were unfaithful and destroyed your marriage in the process.

What if someone is in prison for murder and now they are trying to develop a relationship with God and find healing from their past even though they are more than likely going to spend the rest of their life in prison? Is it even possible for them to be free? Yes, a person can still be free in soul and spirit, even while spending their daily life imprisoned. Actually, I have seen men and women in prison who are more free than some I know who are living in society. True freedom is *inside of us,* not around us.

We should never be afraid to face the truth about our sin,

asking God and the people we have hurt to forgive us. Doing so is never intended to load us down with guilt and condemnation, but rather to set us free. Realizing how much God has forgiven us and the greatness of His mercy brings us closer to Him. Truly, His grace is amazing!

My father repented of his sinful life and received Jesus into his heart at the age of eighty-three, and even after all the horrific and painful things he had done to me and many others, I can say that I know with certainty that God completely forgave him.

The psalmist David, a man who was extremely close to God, committed adultery and murder, and for a year he ran from his actions by ignoring what he had done and their consequences. Finally, after being confronted by Nathan the prophet, David sincerely repented (2 Samuel 12). Part of repentance is honestly facing and admitting our actions and how they affected all who were involved.

David admitted that before he confessed (faced truth), he felt as if his bones were wasting away, and he groaned day and night. That sounds like a man who is miserable in his soul. David was the king; he could do anything he wanted to do and go anywhere he wanted to go, and yet he was not free until he faced truth and took responsibility for his actions (Psalm 32:3–4). But after he confessed, facing truth about all that he had done, God instantly forgave him, and the iniquity and the guilt were dealt with (Psalm 32:5).

David asked God for mercy and stated that he was conscious of his transgression. He wasn't hiding or running any longer (Psalm 51:1–3). He said that God desires truth in the inner being (Psalm 51:6). Facing truth—whether it is the truth about something that has been done to us or something that we have done to someone else or against God—is the key to the healing of the soul and being set free from the past.

There is nothing we cannot be forgiven for. No amount of sin is too much for God to forgive.

> Where sin increased *and* abounded, grace (God's unmerited favor) has surpassed it *and* increased the more *and* superabounded (Romans 5:20).

God's grace—His undeserved favor—is greater than any sin we or anyone else could ever commit.

The Roadblock of Blame

The roadblock of blaming others for my misery and problems was a big one for me. Blaming is in itself a method of running away from reality. As long as we are blaming anyone or anything for our own bad behavior, we will never break free from it. We have to take ownership of our behavior. Own it and become responsible so God can set you free from it.

I became angry each time I didn't get my way, and I blamed others, thinking that if they would just do what I wanted them to do, then I wouldn't get angry. Now, when I think about it, I realize how foolish that was, but at the time it was simply a mechanism I had developed that helped me run from my own problems.

The blame game began in the Garden of Eden (Genesis 3) and has never ceased since then. It can be very interesting to begin observing how often we, as well as others, avoid responsibility for our mistakes and behaviors through blaming.

If I trip in the dark on a rug, I may blame Dave for not leaving the lights on. If Dave almost runs into someone who is backing out of a parking space, it is always their fault for not paying attention to what they were doing. On and on the list goes of things we blame on other people, and most of the time we do it without even realizing what we are doing. Blaming quickly becomes an excuse for us as human beings to not take responsibility for our own actions.

Things like tripping over a rug or almost hitting someone backing out of a parking space are minor examples, and although they may not cause major problems in our lives, they do keep us in the mode of not facing the truth about our behaviors. Most of us have bigger problems than rugs and parking spaces that we need to confront, so let's all make a commitment to face truth and enjoy the freedom that God gives us as a result. Simply saying, "That was totally my fault, and I'm sorry I did it," sets us free and enriches our relationships.

The Roadblock of Excuses

Making excuses for our wrong behavior is a major roadblock to our progress that has to be confronted and moved out of the way. I once heard that excuses are reasons stuffed with lies. In other words, our excuses excuse our behavior as a result of us lying to ourselves about what we did or why we did it. George Washington Carver said, "Ninety-nine percent of failures comes from people who have the habit of making excuses."[21]

I'm sure you have heard the phrase *That is an empty excuse*. And that is exactly what our excuses are. They have no truth in them, and they carry no weight with God. We will find real freedom if we learn to simply say, "I'm sorry and there is no excuse for my behavior." When we can say that and mean it, it sets us free and goes a long way in helping the people we have hurt to forgive us.

> *Learn to say, "I'm sorry and there is no excuse for my behavior."*

The excuses we can come up with are endless, but they are all simply ways to avoid taking responsibility for our actions, and until we do that, there is no healing.

CHAPTER 16

The Roadblock of Self-Pity

As Christians we should never feel sorry for ourselves. The moment we do so we lose our energy, we lose the will to fight and the will to live and are paralyzed.

—Martyn Lloyd-Jones

A Cherokee was teaching his grandson about a battle that goes on in every human being. He said to the young man, "The battle is between two wolves. One wolf is slothful, cowardly, vain, arrogant, and full of self-pity, sorrow, regret, envy, and anger. The other wolf is diligent, courageous, humble, benevolent, and full of compassion, joy, empathy, and faith." Then there was silence.

The grandson thought about the wolves for a moment and then asked his grandfather, "Which wolf wins?"

The Cherokee elder replied, "The one you feed."[22]

I had many reasons, like some of you do, to feel sorry for myself, but my self-pity was a roadblock to the healing of my soul and to living the best life that was available to me. It was such a huge problem for me (as it is for many people), so I want to dedicate an entire chapter to it. Self-pity won't go away on its own. We have to stop feeding it, and that means we need to stop giving in to it.

I learned that just because my enemy, the devil, was inviting me to a pity party, it didn't mean I had to attend. He will offer us many reasons why we should attend by reminding us of all that we do not have in life and tempting us to compare ourselves with other people who seem to have better lives than we do.

I pray that after reading and meditating on the material in this chapter, you will firmly decide to never waste another hour in self-pity, let alone an entire day, or perhaps even days at a time. The days I wasted feeling sorry for myself are far too many to count. They are days I can never get back, because once a day is gone, we never get to go back and do it over. We can, however, learn from our mistakes and make better choices in the future.

Has Self-Pity Ever Helped You?

The truth is that self-pity never helped me even one tiny bit. It didn't help me change anything or make any progress. It never changed the people around me, many of whom I was sure were the source of my pitiful feelings. It drained me of energy, stole any hope I might have had of enjoying anything, and prevented God from helping me. Self-pity leaves us feeling hopeless, and that is one of the worst feelings in the world. It leads to depression and prevents us entirely from seeing the good things that we do have. Self-pity is actually bragging to ourselves about how bad we have

Self-pity is bragging to yourself about how bad you have it in life.

it in life. It sounds something like this: "My life is worse than that of anyone I know. I have it so bad. I don't know how anyone can have it this bad and survive. Nobody understands how I feel and nobody even cares." It is time to start bragging about the good things and asking God to take care of the bad.

Self-pity is an enemy and should be treated as such. We would never knowingly open the door and invite a thief into our home, and yet we do open the door to self-pity and other destructive attitudes that are definitely thieves.

Self-pity comes from an unwillingness to accept a situation or circumstance in your life. It often develops when there are things that we want but cannot have or things we don't want and cannot get rid of. It is a feeling that you are a victim of something or someone. It is fed by meditating over and over on your challenges, difficulties, and problems in life and by comparing your life with someone you think has it better than you do. *Are you feeding the wrong wolf?*

Anyone who is a child of God has seeds of goodness and right behavior in their spirit. They have the ability to enjoy daily life and be thankful for what they do have instead of being resentful about what they do not have. We have Jesus, and all good things are found in Him. He is in us and we are in Him. The seeds of an amazing life are in us, but they won't grow if we continue hindering them from blossoming with destructive attitudes like self-pity.

The apostle Peter said that when we are born again, we are born into an ever-living hope (1 Peter 1:3). In other words, we are never without hope, so God has given us the tools to resist self-pity any time it tries to pay us a visit. Hope is the positive expectation that something good is going to happen to us at any moment. That kind of positive attitude cannot coexist with self-pity.

Instead of feeding the bad wolf, we can choose to feed the good one, the one that makes us thankful, joyful, and helpful to others, all the while trusting God to help us with any difficulty we have.

You Can Have Pity or Power

One Sunday, Dave was watching a football game and certainly seemed to be enjoying himself, the kids were outside playing, and I could faintly hear the sounds of laughter in the yard. I should have been happy that my family was enjoying their day, but instead I was feeling sorry for myself because I was working, which, by the way, was my choice. I was addicted to self-pity, so I actually created circumstances that gave me a reason to be miserable.

I remember I was cleaning house and thinking, *It must be nice to sit and enjoy yourself or be playing outside in the sunshine, but someone has to do the work around here, and it is always me!* The more that kind of thinking turned around and around in my mind, the more I fed the bad wolf and sank into a pit of despair. I cleaned house every day, and I can assure you that I wasn't cleaning because the house was dirty; I was doing it hoping to make Dave feel sorry for me and stop watching football and . . . do what? The odd thing is that when I look back, I don't even know what I wanted him to do, but I do know that I didn't want him to enjoy himself. You see, people who are miserable want others to be miserable, too. They actually resent people who are joyful.

I know that sounds terribly morbid, but facing the truth about my self-pity and what was behind it did eventually set me free from it. I had a terribly wounded soul that resulted from being abused by others and I was in desperate need of healing, but I didn't know how or where to get it. I guess that at that point in my life I didn't even fully recognize that I had a problem, because I was still in the "blaming others" stage in life.

I spent a couple of hours loudly cleaning the house, banging drawers and doors, hoping that Dave would ask me what was wrong, and when he failed to do so, I ended up sitting on the bathroom floor, crying and totally absorbed in self-pity. This scene was not a new one. The floor I sat on may have been located in a different place, but the event was the same. I wasn't getting my way, so I felt sorry for myself.

Sometime during one of my pity parties, I heard God speak in my spirit and say, "You can be pitiful or powerful, but you can't be both. Which one will you choose?" This word from God is one of the most powerful things that God has ever said to me. There are many others, but this ranks among the top "words in due season" that have helped set me free. I was being confronted with a choice

> *You can be pitiful or powerful, but you can't be both.*

and it was up to me. Which wolf was I going to feed? Would I feed the good one or the bad one?

We don't have two wolves living inside of us as the story suggests, but we do have two sides to our nature. We have the fleshly nature that is sense and reason without the Holy Spirit. It is depraved to the maximum degree and totally self-absorbed. We also have a new nature, recreated in the image of God. It is good to the maximum degree. Each day we feed one or the other, and the one we feed the most is the one that becomes the strongest.

By the time God spoke to me about being pitiful or powerful, I was already teaching a small home Bible study every week and truly wanted to make progress in my walk and relationship with God. However, I had many roadblocks in my path that I needed to recognize and deal with. They were all destructive, but self-pity was one of the worst.

God was offering me a life-changing choice, and it was one that only I could make. If I wanted to experience His power in my life, then with His help, I had to give up self-pity. It might seem that the choice would be obvious. After all, who would choose self-pity when power was being offered as an alternative? But people make that choice every day, and it is because they have wallowed in pity for so long that although they hate it, they also find a certain comfort in it. You know what I mean, don't you? You have had a really bad week, month, or year, or maybe even a really bad life. All of your family is gone, and you are home alone. A mountain of laundry awaits you. You make yourself a cup of coffee, and of course you can't eat the cupcake you would love to have because, poor you, you gain weight easily and already need to lose twenty pounds. Admit it: it feels a bit comforting to sit with the warm cup in your hand and think about how bad you have it in life. After all, nobody else thinks about you...right?

It may feel temporarily good to our fleshly nature, but not only is it useless, it's debilitating. It paralyzes us and prevents any progress in life. It is also a sin.

Is Self-Pity a Sin?

Right now, you may not be sure that you are ready to agree with me about self-pity being a sin. You know it is a problem, something that you shouldn't do, but a sin? *Come on, Joyce, isn't that a bit harsh?* I had to face this question myself many years ago, and as I looked for the sin of self-pity, I couldn't find it listed that way anywhere in the Bible. Then God led me to Galatians, where we find a list of the works of the flesh—one of which is idolatry. It is listed along with adultery, witchcraft, anger, envy, murder, and selfish ambition, to name just a few (Galatians 5:19–21).

As I pondered what I felt God was showing me, I tried to disagree with Him a little. *Well, Lord, idolatry is the worship of idols, not self-pity.* And that is when my eyes were opened to the awfulness of the sin of self-pity. It is idolatry because we are turning inward and idolizing ourselves. Everything in our life is about how we have been treated badly, how much we are missing in life, how hard life is for us, what others have that we don't have, and on and on. God wants us to have pity and compassion for others in their pain and misfortune. But I had perverted that wonderful ability from God to reach out and relieve the suffering of others into reaching in and closing myself off from others while I wallowed in a cloud of gloom and negativity.

Yes, self-pity is a sin, and like any other sin, we need to admit it and repent of it. By the way, I just took a little break from my writing and made a cup of coffee, and I am having the cupcake this time (at least half of it, and let me say it is a carrot muffin, so that makes it somewhat "legal" because it has a vegetable in it). I can eat it now because instead of starting my day feeling sorry for myself because I gain weight easily and need to lose twenty pounds, I now walk five miles every morning while I pray and give thanks to God, and I have lost the twenty pounds! Giving up self-pity has wonderful side effects that you don't want to miss.

The temptation to sin will always come, and that is the reason God has given us the fruit of self-control (Galatians 5:22–23). I am still tempted at times to feel sorry for myself when I am having a difficult day, and yes, Dave still watches football, but things have gotten better. He also does dishes now and at times even does laundry while I sit and watch television. God does indeed do amazing things! Like anyone else, I have to resist any temptation to sin, and some days I have to resist the temptation to feel sorry for myself again and again until I gain the victory one more time. But I have come a long way, and I intend to keep going forward one day at a time.

Two of the antidotes for the sickness of self-pity are being aggressively thankful and doing things for others, because when we do this, it helps us keep our minds off of ourselves. Being realistic about our expectations is helpful. If you are going for perfection, you are headed for a lot of disappointment, because nobody is perfect and nobody has a perfect life. We all have things we have to deal with that are unpleasant, and expecting everything to be fun and easy only sets us up for disappointment.

Another wonderful ointment for self-pity is to simply get up and go out and do something. Even something very simple, like going out in the yard or taking short walk, can break the cycle of it. And one thing that works every time is finding something that makes you laugh. And don't you dare think right now, *Ugh, you have got to be kidding, Joyce. There is nothing in my life to laugh about.*

It is time to give up all the excuses and knock the roadblocks in life out of the way so you can move forward. Healing for your soul and an enjoyable life are waiting for you on the other side of the roadblocks. Being free from self-pity, or any of the other roadblocks I have mentioned, certainly may not be the total answer to healing your wounded soul—you may need other help and more time—but it is certainly a great beginning and can only make things better for you. Trust God for total healing, because Jesus can heal you everywhere you hurt!

CHAPTER 17

Stand Up for Yourself

*Courage is contagious. When a brave man takes a stand,
the spines of others are often stiffened.*

—Billy Graham

History is filled with stories of people who took a stand for what is right and changed history because of it. People like Martin Luther King Jr., Eleanor Roosevelt, Rosa Parks, Alice Paul, Susan B. Anthony, and many others. You might be used to change history for many, but if not, you can at least be someone who changes your own history. Your painful past doesn't ever have to be your destiny—you can take a stand against the wrong behavior of other people who have harmed you, and when you do, you will feel empowered, rather than merely feeling like a helpless victim.

People who are being abused or mistreated need to be courageous, speak up, and take a stand to protect themselves. Most abusive people will back down when confronted. I am familiar with a case in which, for years, the man in the home has been controlling, demeaning, and very quick to get angry when things don't go his way. His wife is meek and tends to be fearful, so she simply put up with his behavior for many years. She has finally started standing up to him, and although they have a long way to go, he is treating her somewhat better. He has been getting counseling regarding his anger issue, and he actually admitted in a counseling session that since she is no longer willing to put up with his bad behavior and is confronting him, he is treating her better.

Most controlling people will do whatever others are willing to put up with, and although it would be much better and say more good things about their character if they treated others well because it is the right thing to do, they usually don't. Abusers usually disrespect people who meekly put up with their bad behavior. A part of them actually wants someone to confront them. They may react badly at first, but in the long run it is the only way they will stop abusing.

Obviously, there are people who become even more angry and violent when confronted, and if that is the case, the best option is to get away from them. I can't imagine how much different our lives would have been if my mother had confronted my father, but since she never did, she hurt not only herself but also my brother and me. Her only excuse was that she was afraid. Fear is a feeling that serves to keep us from making progress or doing the thing we know that we should do, but we can learn to stand up for ourselves, even if we have to "do it afraid."

Abraham Lincoln said, "Be sure your feet are in the right place and then stand firm."[23] It is important that we take a stand, but it needs to be done in a proper way. I have known people who, while in the process of taking a stand for themselves, end up hurting others even worse than they have been hurt. I was one of those people for a while, until I learned to do things God's way instead of my own way.

I determined that nobody would ever push me around or abuse me once I got away from my father, but in the process I became rebellious and controlling. I started changing eventually, but it was only after Dave began confronting me. He read a book about caring enough to confront, and God used it to let him know the time had come for him to take a stand.

Right timing is critically important. We should always pray and look for the right time and place to confront. Dave prayed for me for many years because he knew I behaved badly because I had been deeply hurt, and I truly believe that his prayers helped prepare my heart to change. God was working in me and teaching me, and I had come to the point where I truly wanted to change, but I can honestly say that Dave confronting me was the thing that I needed to make me take my problems seriously enough to start doing something about them.

One of the things I realized that helped me was that I was trying to make Dave pay for what other men had done to me, and that was totally unfair to him. I was afraid that if I let him exercise any authority as the head of our home, he would take advantage of me as all other men had done, and I wasn't going to let that happen ever again. I finally learned that only God could pay me back for the pain in my past and that I needed to believe that Dave wasn't like the men who had hurt me.

Stand up for yourself, but do it in the right way. Don't become ungodly while trying to deal with the ungodly behavior of others. I know a girl in her twenties who grew up in a home with an angry and explosive father who was very controlling. She initially was afraid of his anger and became nervous and anxious because she didn't feel that she was in a safe environment, but eventually she found her voice. She certainly no longer lets anyone control her, but she has become excessive in her attitude and often reacts as if someone were trying to control her even if they express an opinion that is different than hers. She feels that women in general are marginalized and undervalued in the workplace, and she is determined to help right some of the wrongs. Her motive is good, but her methods are not. She is becoming a radical feminist who views many things as mistreatment, while, in fact, that is not the case at all. She behaves as if women should have *special rights* rather than *equal rights*!

> Don't become ungodly while trying to deal with the ungodly behavior of others.

When a woman has been seriously mistreated, it is unlikely that she has the ability to view things and people in a balanced way as long as she is judging them through her pain. We need God's Word to guide us into what is right, and we need a willing heart that will be obedient to it and view it as the supreme authority in our lives. The only way I learned what right behavior is came through studying God's Word. We don't always want to do what is right, but if what we want to do or feel like doing is not in agreement with God's Word, then we can submit to God's ways, knowing that in the end, they are always right and produce the best result.

Follow God, Not Man

We have many good examples of men and women in the Bible who stood up for themselves. Daniel was a young man who trusted God and prayed three times daily with his windows open. The king gave an order that no one could pray to any god but him or they would be punished by being put into a lions' den. Daniel went to his room and opened the windows and continued to pray as he had done before. He was put into the lions' den; however, God was with him and delivered him safely. He sent an angel to shut the lions' mouths so they could not hurt Daniel (Daniel 6:7–22).

The apostles were forbidden to preach in the name of Jesus on the threat of being jailed and beaten, but they preached anyway. They were beaten and they were put in jail, but God sent an angel to release them miraculously and the jailer and his household became believers in God (Acts 16). If you do things God's way, you can be used by Him to help many other people who may be going through the same type of pain that you once did.

Rosa Parks, a black seamstress, was required by law to give up her seat on the bus and let a white man have it, but she refused. Her refusal spurred the civil rights movement in the United States, which was led by Martin Luther King Jr. Rosa followed her heart instead of the demands of men, and the results of her bold actions are still bearing witness today.

The Stress-Reducing Power of Being Assertive

I recently came across a story about assertiveness that I found interesting. The director of a small library in the Midwest, Marcia (not her real name), says she was meek and mild for many years: "I let people walk all over me, and I ended up being really unhappy a lot of the time."

But one day she stood up for herself and everything changed.

Marcia had made a small work error, and a library trustee known for her bullying manner sent a strongly worded reprimand to Marcia's personal email address, copying it to the entire board. Marcia acknowledged the error and apologized for her mistake, and then she asked that the trustee not copy the entire board on such an email just to make her look bad. Well, the next day, this bully of a boss showed up at the library and reprimanded Marcia in person, in front of her entire staff.

"I snapped," Marica says. "I stood up and said, 'As far as I'm concerned, this conversation is done. You've made yourself perfectly clear. I apologized. It's over.'"

And that is when an interesting thing happened: the woman stepped back and said, "Well, I guess now we have a direction," meaning that Marcia finally showed she had the assertiveness necessary for the job.

Marcia has never been the same since. She has discovered the power of asserting herself and freed herself forever from being bullied, backstabbed, or walked on.[24]

Although meekness is a quality that Jesus demonstrated, and one that He encourages each of us to develop, a true godly meekness is quite different from what the world calls meek. True meekness is strength under control. It means that we have the power to do something, but we won't move to do so unless God guides us to. Much of what the world calls meekness is just weakness and fear.

Going along to get along sounds like a peaceful approach to relationships, and while that may be accurate at times, in reality, learning to be assertive when we need to, ask for what we want and need, say no when necessary, and demand due respect is more effective and less stressful. When we take a stand for ourselves, we are setting boundaries.

When we stand up for ourselves we are not trying to control what other people do, but rather we are controlling what they do to us. We are saying by our actions and words that we will no longer remain inactive while they bully or demean us. We are letting others know that we respect and value ourselves and that we expect them to do the same.

When you take a stand for yourself, you are setting boundaries.

If you are going to confront someone about something, I don't recommend doing it in an email or even on the phone if at all possible. Face-to-face is best, because that way our demeanor, facial expressions, and body language can be seen as our words are being heard. Something firm can be said with a smile and be easier to receive than if it is said with a scowl on our face. It can be said while comfortably seated in a chair and come across very differently than if it is said while standing stiffly with hands on hips. Keep your voice tones as kind as possible, but also be firm and determined. The Bible states that "a gentle answer turns away wrath, but a harsh word stirs up anger" (Proverbs 15:1 NIV).

It is usually best not to confront or be too assertive when we're angry, because then the anger we are feeling, rather than the Holy Spirit, is controlling us. Waiting to confront a situation doesn't always work, but when possible, I have found it to be best.

When we know we are being mistreated or disrespected and we do nothing, it creates stress because we know it isn't right, and we actually don't like ourselves very much because we are allowing it. Doing things that our heart doesn't agree with always creates stress, whether we are doing something that we know is wrong or not doing something that we know would be right.

The First Step May Be the Most Difficult

If you have a history of not speaking up or just going along to get along, taking the first step toward being more assertive and letting your voice be heard probably will be very difficult. You may not even get a good result the first time you do it. I had an employer who was very controlling, and when I finally confronted him after several years of not doing so, he became extremely angry and stormed out of the restaurant where we were. In this instance, my confrontation didn't change him, but it did convince me that I needed to work someplace else, and that is what I did. My confrontation may not have changed him, but it did change me and actually set me on the path in life that has led me into the ministry I have today.

Don't let the fear of taking a stand hold you back from being all you can be and doing all that you can do. You will never be fulfilled and satisfied if you don't fulfill your destiny. You are far too valuable

> *You are far too valuable to let anyone abuse you.*

to passively let anyone abuse or misuse you. It is time to take a stand!

CHAPTER 18

Establish Boundaries— Don't Build Walls

You get what you tolerate.

—Henry Cloud

Are you resentful because you feel that people take advantage of you? Perhaps all you need to do is establish some boundaries. A boundary is like a fence that protects your property. If I have no fence and the dogs in the neighborhood relieve themselves in my yard while taking their morning walk, I can't blame the dog. I need to either clean up after them without complaining or put up a fence.

I remember complaining to God about the employer I mentioned who was controlling me, and God surprised me by telling me that I was just as guilty as he was because although he was controlling me, I was letting him do it. Ouch! It is important for us to establish boundaries in all areas of our lives. Some boundaries we set are for ourselves: they may be boundaries for our eating habits, budget, how much we work versus how much we rest, and other things that help us have healthy disciplines in our daily lives. Other boundaries that we set are for people. These boundaries prevent us from being hurt, and they help others realize that if they want a relationship with us, they won't be allowed to take advantage of us in the process.

Maybe you are a helpful person who has a kind heart but you need to be careful that you don't develop a habit of taking care of other people who don't make any effort to take care of themselves. Are you worn-out from trying to help someone who doesn't want to be helped? Have you allowed a person to become so dependent on you to provide for and help them that now you resent them but continue doing what they ask you to do? If you said yes to any of these questions, it means you need boundaries in those relationships.

God's Word teaches us to be thoughtful, but it urges us to exercise *wise* thoughtfulness (Proverbs 1:3). It actually says we are to use the discipline of wise thoughtfulness. In other words, you may want to help someone but need to discipline yourself not to, because deep in your heart, you know it will ultimately be better for them if you don't. Parents who help their children too much and who do too much for them, always rescuing them when they have a problem, are not helping them prepare for the future. They are actually enabling them to be irresponsible adults.

Anytime someone asks you for something, whether it is a favor, help with a project, or financial help, they want you to say yes to their request, but it is not good to always tell people what they want to hear. When we do that we may be in danger of becoming people pleasers instead of God pleasers. When we are asked to do something for another person, we should give heartfelt and honest responses. It is important for each of us to learn to follow our heart, and that means to follow the guidance of God in all things. God's Word teaches us to speak the truth in love (Ephesians 4:15), because a dishonest relationship is an unhealthy one.

The more God works in our lives and heals our wounded souls, the more we enjoy helping other people, and while that is good, we must be careful not to let people take advantage of us. I realized several years ago that I had several one-sided relationships, ones in which I did all the giving and the other party did all of the taking, and I decided that I needed to set some boundaries.

I will always help people in need, but if it becomes excessive or I feel that I am being used without also being loved and cared for, then I stop. We should never give merely to get something back, but all relationships need boundaries in order for them to be healthy. Even God reaches a point in His relationship with us where He is no longer willing to do all the giving while we show no interest in spending time with Him or serving Him in any way. He is a loving and generous Father who never stops loving us, and while we are in the baby stage of our relationship with Him, He gives and gives and gives, but eventually it isn't good for us to not start giving back.

Love reproves and chastises in addition to helping and giving. We truly do not love another person if we let them take advantage of us. God confronts us for our own good, and He does it because He loves us.

> Those whom I [dearly and tenderly] love, I tell their faults and convict *and* convince *and* reprove and chasten [I discipline and instruct them] (Revelation 3:19).

Healthy boundaries are safety nets for us and other people, but we do need to be sure that we truly are setting boundaries, not building walls. Most fences have a gate in them, and if they don't, they are no longer a fence but a prison. When a fence has a gate, we can get

We truly do not love another person if we let them take advantage of us.

out if we want to and let someone in if we want to, but walls have no gates. They wall others out of our life, but they also wall us in.

A healthy boundary in relationships might look something like this in our thinking: *I've been hurt a lot in my life, and I want to protect myself and have relationships with safe people. Therefore, I am going to use discernment concerning the people I get involved with, and if a person begins to take advantage of me, I will confront them. If they continue to do it, I will open the gate and let them out of my life.*

In contrast, a wall in a relationship might look like this in our thinking: *I've been hurt in the past, and nobody is ever going to hurt me again. I will take care of myself and protect myself. I won't let myself get close to anyone, and that way they can't hurt me.* In this case, I may think I have established a boundary, but in reality it is a wall.

One of the first things I did for years after I had gotten away from my father was to quickly erect a wall in my heart if anyone I knew hurt me at all. I could actually feel the walls go up, and I thought they made me safe. Finally, with God's help, I realized that although He does want us to establish healthy boundaries, only He can be a true wall of protection around us.

If you have built walls in your heart to keep others from hurting you, only you can tear them down. If you don't, you can never love or really receive love in return. I cannot promise you that you will never be hurt, but I can promise that even if you are, God will always heal you. Since there are no perfect people and we all have weaknesses, it is not possible to be in relationships and never experience being hurt or disappointed.

Inner Vows

We can make vows with ourselves that need to be broken. I had vowed that nobody would ever hurt me again and nobody would control me or tell me what to do. Nobody would take advantage of me, and I would take care of myself and never let myself get into a position of needing anyone. Obviously, if we try to live with that kind of an attitude, we cannot have any relationships. We all get hurt from time to time. Even very good and well-meaning people hurt one another. We cannot live in society and never have anyone tell us what to do or give us any direction, but many people today are trying to do just that, and the world around us is filled with rebellion and lawlessness. And, like it or not, we do need each other. God has created us in such a way that we are to work together, not isolate ourselves and be totally independent from one another. If you have been hurt and disappointed and because of it have decided that you don't need anybody, I understand how you feel because I was the same way. But that attitude will need to change in order for you to have a healthy, healed soul. We are not created to be alone.

I had to break the wrong vows I had made to myself, and I did so by praying and confessing that my attitude was wrong and asking God to help me have healthy boundaries, not walls. When someone hurts me, even now I can feel a wall beginning to go up in my heart, but I don't permit it to remain because I know it is not God's will.

Isolation

When we have walls in our heart and refuse to let people in, those walls become hindrances that actually prevent us from growing spiritually in our relationship with God. It is not possible to have a good relationship with God and isolate ourselves from people. We might say that God is a people person. He loves people and wants to show His love for them through us. I have found that the Bible is a great book about relationships. It is about our relationship with God, with ourselves, and with our fellow man. Part of the process of working out our salvation and experiencing restoration is cooperating with the Holy Spirit so that all of these relationships are healed and healthy. While there may be some people we can never have relationships with because they continue to be abusive, we must not wall all people out of our lives out of fear. God wants us to live in community with others, loving and being loved, giving and receiving forgiveness, enjoying one another and bearing with one another's weaknesses (Galatians 6:1–3).

I often say when I'm teaching that in the early years of my healing journey, I got along well with everyone, wasn't quick to get angry, was patient, kind, and loving—as long as nobody was home. But when the people came home, it was a different story. You may relate well to what I am saying. I was a stay-at-home mom during a few of those years. During the day, when Dave was at work and my children were in school, I listened to worship music or teachings while doing my household duties, and all was peaceful and good. But when my children came home and started making noise or doing things that aggravated me, I turned into another person. I suddenly was not patient, slow to anger, kind, or loving.

Some of us choose isolation rather than taking a chance on relationships after we've been hurt, but we cannot make spiritual progress toward becoming like Christ if we do that. For example, we can never learn patience if everything goes our way quickly.

We can never learn to love unlovely people or those with habits that annoy us if we are never around them. God uses people with rough edges to sand the rough edges off of us.

> *God uses people with rough edges to sand the rough edges off of us.*

Being alone in life may seem to be easier, but it is also emptier. When we are alone, we don't have to face the truth about who we really are. You may purchase an orange that looks beautiful on the outside, but when you squeeze it or cut into it you find that it is dry and tasteless. Only truth makes us free, and it is imperative to our spiritual growth that we have the "squeezes" in life that other people provide.

It is not good to be alone. God created Eve because He said it was not good for the man to be alone. Even God is not alone because He is a Trinity—Father, Son, and Holy Spirit.

It is easy when we are alone to be blind to our faults because there is no one to confront us. There is nothing to squeeze us so that we can see what we are like under pressure. A pastor once told me, "Joyce, you will never know anyone fully until you see how they respond in all kinds of situations." And I have definitely found that to be true.

Dave teasingly says that God put him in my life to crucify my flesh, and he is more right than he may think he is. When Dave and I got married, he was everything that I was not. As I saw daily how he responded to situations and people compared to how I did, it was a continual reminder that I had problems and needed help to change.

I was impatient and he was very patient, so his patience (which I viewed as slowness) irritated me. I made very quick decisions, and he took a long time to make them, so that was a problem for me. The list could go on and on, but my point is that I would never have changed had I not been with Dave and lots of other people, many of whom irritated and annoyed me. Finally, I had to ask the question, *Are people really annoying, or am I too hard to please?* It was a painful, tearful, and difficult day when I finally admitted that I had a big problem and that I was almost impossible to please. But it was also the day I started to make some progress.

> *Are people really annoying, or am I just too hard to please?*

I urge you not to isolate yourself because you just don't like dealing with the messiness of relationships. Yes, there may be pain, but in the end it is worth it.

Alone in a Room Filled with People

Have you ever been in a room filled with people and felt alone? Most of us have, and it can happen for different reasons. It may be simply that we do not know anyone in the room. Of course, our temptation is to wait for someone to come and talk with us or be friendly toward us, but someone who is confident and secure will take the initiative and reach out to others.

We may also feel alone around people if we have our walls up for fear of being rejected. Those who have experienced a lot of rejection in their lives often fear being rejected so much that either they isolate themselves or their fears create behavior traits in them that actually drive others away.

Janet was a woman who wanted to get involved at her church and be included in the social events that took place. She joined a study group and began noticing that when they took trips, they usually didn't invite her. This same type of thing had happened to her over and over in her life, and she didn't want it to keep happening, so she summoned the courage to ask one of the women in the group who seemed to have no difficulty in expressing her feelings why she was not invited.

The woman was honest with her and told her that she suffocated people, because if anyone was friendly with her, she tried to attach herself to them in an out-of-balance way. Although this was painful for Janet to hear and it took some time and counseling to fully understand what the woman was saying, the confrontation did help her to stop blaming and start asking herself some questions: *Why am I so suffocating? Am I really out of balance in my approach to relationships?* The end result was that Janet learned she was so afraid of being rejected because of the pain of her past, that when anyone seemed even a little friendly to her, she wanted to be with them all the time due to fear of losing the relationship.

I know a woman who is like this, and although she is in many ways a kind, giving, and lovely woman, she also inserts herself into personal areas of the lives of the people who befriend her, and she does it in a way that is inappropriate and actually rude. Because she is this way, people tend to avoid her. She does not know how to respect other people's boundaries, and that can be as much of a problem as if she had no boundaries of her own.

CHAPTER 19

Become Your Own Best Ally

Like the fairy tale suggests, the "mirror, mirror on the wall" shows us the face of our enemy ... we defeat ourselves far more than we are defeated by external circumstances.
—John Maxwell

We all want people to approve of us and be for us rather than against us, and some are, but we also find that some are not. When that is the case, it can be painful, and if we have experienced too many people who are not or were not for us, it can leave wounds in our souls that need to be healed. Even the disapproval of one person, if it is a parent or a spouse, can deeply wound a person. We desire the love of our family and close friends, and not getting it is often devastating to some people. I meet and talk with people who are forty or fifty years old who are still struggling with dysfunctional lifestyles because they had a parent who rejected or showed continual disapproval of them.

The apostle Paul encouraged the Romans with these words:

> If God is for us, who [can be] against us? [Who can be our foe, if God is on our side?] (Romans 8:31).

The psalmist David said:

> The Lord is on my side; I will not fear. What can man do to me? (Psalm 118:6).

Both of these men, who were used greatly by God, encountered many people who were not for them. They were comforted by and comforted others with the knowledge that although we will deal with people who are not for us and do not approve of us, God is always for us, and He is on our side in our times of struggle, pain, and challenge.

It is time that we make a decision to agree with God rather than agreeing with our enemies. Perhaps you have formed an opinion of yourself based on what unkind people have said or thought about you, or how they have treated you. If so, that is a mistake that needs to be corrected. It is time for you to be *for you*, and that simply means it is time for you to be a friend to yourself, to be your own best ally, and to learn to love yourself in a godly way.

No matter how much God wants to do for and through us, He cannot do any of it unless we come into agreement with Him, and that means we agree with His Word. All of His promises become a reality in our lives only if we believe them. If God says we are

> *It is time for you to be a friend to yourself.*

greatly loved and filled with His wisdom, then we are. If He says that we are forgiven and that His plan for our future is good, then it is.

Are You Your Own Worst Enemy?

Perhaps you have listened to other people and their criticisms for so long that you now have a low opinion of yourself. I want to suggest that you take a break from reading and ask how you feel about yourself. Do you like yourself? Do you see and appreciate the talents and abilities that God has given you? Do you know that you are valuable? This morning as I was taking a walk, I asked myself what the most important thing was that God had taught me that has helped me receive healing in my wounded soul, and I knew right away that it was Him teaching me to love and accept myself as His creation and daughter and to become a friend to myself. This has been truly life-changing for me, and I believe it will be for you, too.

I have gone from self-rejection to learning to enjoy myself. I like to be with me. I am going out to lunch today with me. I enjoy spending whole days with me. I pray that you also like to be with you. You might as well learn to be yourself and to love, enjoy, and value yourself, because you will always be you. We all change as we grow in becoming more like Christ, but there are things about ourselves that we will need to accept even if those things are not what we would have chosen for ourselves. If you are taller than you wish you were, you will always be tall; if you are shorter in stature, you will always be short. You can wear taller shoes, but eventually you have to take them off and then you are short once again.

I used to wish I had a sweeter voice and personality, and it caused me to compare myself with other women who were what I thought I wanted to be. Hopefully my personality is a little sweeter these days, but my voice is still deep and gets attention. I usually don't say anything very quietly. I wanted to have longer, thicker hair like a friend of mine, but it is still short and baby-fine in texture. We can waste our lives not liking one thing or another about ourselves, but it is much wiser to focus on your strengths and all the amazing qualities that God has given you.

Learning to like yourself and be your own best ally is one of the best decisions you can ever make. No matter how many people love and admire you, if you don't like yourself, you will never be happy. Let me ask you a question: If you are feeling bad about yourself, is it because of what someone else thinks of you or is it because of what you think of yourself? I truly believe that if we live in the reality of who God says we are, we can easily overcome any negative opinions that other people may have.

The apostle Paul was frequently criticized, but he seemed to value God's opinion of him more than he did anyone else. He said:

> But [as for me personally] it matters very little to me that I should be put on trial by you [on this point], *and* that you or any other human tribunal should investigate *and* question *and* cross-question me. I do not even put myself on trial *and* judge myself.
>
> I am not conscious of anything against myself, *and* I feel blameless; but I am not vindicated *and* acquitted before God on that account. It is the Lord [Himself] Who examines *and* judges me (1 Corinthians 4:3–4).

These Scriptures have helped me many times when I have been feeling bad about myself because of the criticism of other people. I have discovered that the only way in life to never be criticized is to do

> *The dread of criticism can be the death of greatness.*

nothing and be nothing, but even then we would be criticized for being lazy and unproductive.

The dread of criticism can be the death of greatness. When we are criticized it is wise to consider whether or not our critic might be right, and if they are, thank them; if they aren't, pray for them.

Make Peace with Yourself

Let me encourage you to make peace with yourself. None of us is all that we wish we were, but we can embrace who we are and go on in life to do great things. God assigns a measure of weakness to each of us so that we will always need to depend on and need Him. There are no perfect people. Paul struggled with his weaknesses until God told him that His strength was perfected in and through them. After that, Paul embraced them and accepted they were part of who he was (2 Corinthians 12:8–9). God's Word never promises us that we can reach a place where we will have no deficits, flaws, or weaknesses, but it does promise us that God will be our strength. Remember that God is not surprised that we have flaws; He knows things about each of us that we have yet to discover, and He loves us unconditionally.

A psychologist I once interviewed said that women needed to make peace with their thighs. So many women have a misconception of what they think they should look like. Most of us are not going to look like the model on the magazine cover whose picture has been airbrushed to perfection or the movie star who is filmed in such a way that none of her flaws are visible. I believe we should take what we have been given by God and make it look the best we can, while refusing to compare ourselves with anyone else. If there is anything you don't like about the way you look and you can do something about it, then do it, but if you can't, make peace with it and enjoy being you. You live with yourself all the time, and if you don't like yourself, you are going to be miserable.

Let's say that a woman's face is covered with freckles and she does not want freckles. Perhaps she has a desire to be an actress but is convinced that her freckles are too big a flaw to be overcome, so she never follows her dream and ends up unfulfilled in life because she isn't doing what she was meant to do. Do you know that one of the most famous actresses I know of had freckles? Her name is Doris Day. She was absolutely beautiful in her movies and no one paid any attention to the freckles. I think nobody noticed them because she didn't make a big deal out of them. She followed her dream and succeeded. Perhaps if we won't focus so much on what we think our flaws are, others won't notice them, either.

As Christians we are taught to be humble, but a person who is truly humble doesn't belittle themselves or think they are not as good as other people. They simply know who they are in Christ and that any good thing they are able to do is a gift from God; they are not above or better than anyone else, but they are not less than them, either. Actually, a truly humble person doesn't spend their time thinking about all that is right with them or all that is wrong with them because they simply don't have their mind on themselves excessively. They are not overly concerned about how they look, what people think of them, or maintaining a position of being first in all things. They are free to be who they are and do their best for God. We are nothing without Christ, but we can do all things through Him! Jesus welcomes flawed people, and He delights in working through them.

The Agony of Self-Doubt

When we have a low opinion of ourselves, we rarely feel qualified to make decisions. We can easily fall into the agony of doubting ourselves about everything we think, feel, and decide. No one is right all the time, but no one is wrong all the time, either, and we need to learn to follow godly wisdom and then trust ourselves to make good decisions.

Do you find yourself making a decision and then wondering excessively whether or not you made the right one? Do you frequently change your mind and find yourself being double-minded, stuck between two decisions and feeling stressed about which one is right? When we need to make decisions, we should ask God to help us decide what is right, and then once we have decided, we should not hesitate and be double-minded about our choice. The apostle James said that if we are filled with self-doubt, we are not able to receive the help we need from God (James 1:5–6). While it is true that not every decision is the right one, the only way we can find out sometimes is to simply start moving forward in the direction we believe is best, and it will soon become clear if we are right or not.

Is the fear of making a wrong decision making you indecisive? Do you realize that to make no decision is still a decision? We don't protect ourselves from making mistakes by refusing to do anything. Even if you do make a mistake, it won't be the end of the world and at least you can learn from it.

> *Is the fear of making a wrong decision making you indecisive?*

Do you find yourself asking too many other people what you should do when you need to make a decision? While it is certainly not wrong and may even be helpful to get an opinion regarding a decision, we must remember that when we ask people what they would do, their advice may be right for them but totally wrong for us. Everyone has varying opinions about many things, and asking too many people can end up causing more confusion rather than helping. At the very least, it can waste a lot of time, because ultimately, you are the one who must make the decision in the end.

If you constantly do what people think you should do instead of following your own heart, you are denying who you are and the right God has given you to make choices of your own.

Trust yourself to be able to follow your heart and to know the best thing that you should do. Never do anything that God's Word doesn't approve of or anything that your conscience tells you is wrong, but always remember that many roads may get you to the same destination, and God has given you the privilege of deciding which road you want to take. The decision you make isn't wrong just because it isn't what someone else would do.

When you are making a life-altering decision, take plenty of time to make it, pray about it, see what God's Word says about it, and follow peace. Believe that you can

> *The decision you make isn't wrong just because it isn't what someone else would do.*

make good decisions. Trust that God is guiding you, and live boldly, without fear.

Make a decision to be your best friend instead of your worst enemy. Don't defeat yourself. God is for you, and He wants you to be for yourself, too. You are a truly wonderful person who has a tremendous amount of potential, so start moving forward and being all you can be.

CHAPTER 20

Healing the Wounds of Codependency

I was your cure, and you were my disease. I was saving you, but you were killing me!

—Author unknown

Nothing is more painful than watching someone you love suffer deeply and, in some cases, do harm to themselves through wrong or addictive behavior. It wounds our own souls to watch the people we love wound theirs. It is always good to try to help the people we care about who are hurting, but when helping them begins to destroy us, then we have to stop.

> *It wounds your soul to watch the people you love wound theirs.*

My brother, who was my only sibling, was an alcoholic and a drug addict and eventually became paranoid schizophrenic due to long-term drug abuse. We tried for many years to help him without permanent success. It seemed that as long as we totally devoted our lives to helping him, he did fairly well, but without constant oversight and supervision he always reverted back to his addictive behaviors. I loved him and wanted more than anything to help him, but I was unable to.

I finally had to realize that trying to cure him was stealing my life. The last time we had him in a treatment program, he left of his own volition and disappeared. Sadly, several months later we got word that he was found dead in an abandoned building. When I heard the news I had a temptation to feel guilty and wonder if I had done enough, but I knew deep in my heart that only he could make the decisions he needed to make and that no one could help him unless he did his part. If someone you love is making bad choices and all of your efforts to help them have not done any good, be careful that you don't take on an exaggerated sense of responsibility, thinking it is your job to rescue them.

Wanting to help someone we love does not mean that we are codependent, but our efforts to help can morph into codependency if we aren't careful. When a person is codependent, it means that their life is controlled by someone else's problems or bad choices. They may never know how any day will go for them because it is dependent on what the troubled person in their life does. I remember numerous times when Dave and I were home and just starting to relax after a challenging day at the office, and I would receive a call letting me know that my brother was in jail or was displaying psychotic behavior and the people he was with didn't know what to do with him. We often had to cancel our plans because of my brother's problems. We should all be willing to change our plans if someone truly needs our help, but if the same person creates the same situation over and over, it is not good.

My brother lived in our home for four years while we tried to help him get his life going in the right direction, and I finally realized that if we are trying to help anyone for four years and they are not any better after all that time, then there is a good chance they don't really intend to change. Many people say they want to change, but they are not willing to do what is required of them. No one can fix someone else's problems for them if that person isn't prepared to do their part.

If you are in a codependent relationship, the hardest thing you may ever do might be to walk away or stop helping. I met a woman recently while shopping, and she told me she had been in a relationship for over six years with a man who had problems with alcohol. She wasn't happy and knew that her life was going nowhere, and she wanted me to give her advice. It also saddened her that they were not married because he wasn't prepared to make a long-term commitment to her. I could tell after just a few minutes of talking to her that she had already had good advice from many people, but she was not yet willing to take any of it. I told her what others were telling her, which was that she needed to get away from him. She said, "I know I should, but I am codependent on him. I'm not happy with him, but I don't know if I can live without him!" She continued wanting me to talk with her, but no matter how many times I told her what she needed to do, her response was always, "I know, but it is just so hard." There was nothing I could do for her.

I wonder how many years she will let him steal her life and make her unhappy before she finally walks away—or, for that matter, will she ever walk away? My mother hated what my father did—his abuse, drinking, and violent behavior—and yet she would never leave him. She loved him, but she hated him. She was addicted to him and the dysfunctional life that she lived with him. She had learned how to function within her dysfunction, and it had become so normal for her that she couldn't imagine anything else.

Deciding when the time is right to distance yourself from someone is a choice that you must make for yourself, and it should be done after much prayer and contemplation. God has called us to help people and to do so even at the cost of self-sacrifice, but He has not called us to live lives in which we are being controlled and manipulated by the poor choices that other people make.

If your soul is being wounded by the bad choices of someone you love, I know how you feel, and I know that the pain is very deep, but if trying to assist them isn't working, perhaps you would help them more if you stopped trying. Sometimes we think we are helping, but in reality we are enabling the person to continue hurting us. If you are not helping them, at least you can help yourself by going on with your life. It is not uncommon for troubled people to never be willing to make a change as long as they have someone who continues rescuing them.

Mothers and Their Children

I have heard that a mother is never happier than her unhappiest child, and I can testify to the truth of that statement. I have four children, and I know how I feel when they are hurting. If you have a child who is addicted to destructive behaviors, only God can get you through the pain and disappointment. People who are in that type of situation consistently tell me that only God gets them through it. He can reach places in the depth of our souls that no one else could ever reach. I urge you to totally rely on Him to guide, heal, and restore you. His grace is sufficient even in situations that are more painful than we could have ever imagined.

Thankfully, with God, we are never without hope, and hope is a great motivator that moves us along in life with an expectation that something good can happen.

> *Hope is a great motivator.*

If you have a child in pain or who needs healing and deliverance in their life, and your soul is weary and wounded from what you have dealt with, I can assure you that God can reach into your soul and refresh and heal you. Spend regular time with the Lord and ask Him to strengthen and heal you.

It is very hard for a mother to watch her children make bad choices and not be able to reach them, knowing that those choices will ultimately bring them pain. God gives each of us free choice, even if the choices we make are not the right ones, and sometimes the only way we learn to do better is by experiencing the painful results of our wrong choices. Sometimes not helping is the most merciful thing we can do.

Don't ever give up on the people you love. Even if all of your efforts to get through to them have failed, remember that God can do in a moment of time what we cannot do in a lifetime. A mother's prayers for her children are very powerful, and even when it looks like nothing is changing, it doesn't mean that God isn't working. It might take a while—perhaps even a long while—to see results, but all things are possible with God!

> God can do in a moment what we cannot do in a lifetime.

Being Out of Control and Loving It

A great deal of our pain and misery is caused by trying to control people and situations that we cannot control. It is usually difficult for most parents to admit they are controlling if they are—and that includes me—but I believe we can learn to be out of control and love it! We can love the freedom it brings us, and I also believe that when we totally turn a situation over to God, He does much more than when we are trying to "help" Him do

His work. Sometimes we think we are helping, but we are actually hindering. But when we cast our care, worry, and anxiety on God, He cares for us (see 1 Peter 5:7).

I recently went through something that was troubling me and stealing my peace, and when I finally faced the real issue behind what was causing my unhappiness, God showed me that I was trying to control what people were doing in a specific situation and I needed to stop. Sometimes I find it difficult to draw the line between being responsible and being controlling, so I continue learning from God in this very important area of life.

I am by nature a responsible person, and I can easily take on a false sense of responsibility. For example, I really want all of my children to take good care of themselves so they protect their health, feel good, and live a long life. Of course, I think I know how they should do it. After all, "Mother knows best," right? I am still learning to not comment when I see them eat things that I know aren't good for them or when I know they are not getting enough sleep. I can ask a few too many questions about whether or not they are being diligent to exercise, get their doctor checkups, and so on.

When I can see that they are becoming impatient with me, I always think and often say, "I am just trying to help you!" I'm sure that sounds familiar if you are a mom. I am learning more and more how to pray and watch God work instead of being too free with my advice, but I still have more to learn.

Giving up control is actually very freeing. The only person God wants us to control is ourselves, and that should be our goal. We don't like it when anyone tries to control us, so how can we expect other people to like it if we do it to them?

I am sure you have heard the statement "Let go and let God be

God," and perhaps you don't want to hear it again, but it is the truth. When we let go, God begins to work. Never stop praying, and if God opens a door for you to give a word of advice at the right time, give it—but don't keep trying to make people listen who don't want to hear you. If you do, it will only steal your peace and joy.

Signs That You Are Helping Too Much

What are the signs that you might be helping or giving too much? There are things that we can and should watch for in our lives and here are a few:

Sign 1: You may be helping too much if you resent what you are doing. I believe that when we are doing what God wants us to do, we should feel peace, not resentment.

Sign 2: If what you are doing is fostering irresponsibility or incompetence, or if it is making the one you are helping too dependent upon you, it is a sign that you are helping too much.

Sign 3: If you have a feeling that you are being manipulated, you are helping too much.

Sign 4: If what you intended as a one-time blessing has become a long-term obligation that is now a burden to you, you might be helping too much.

Sign 5: If you continue to say yes to the person you are helping when you know in your heart you should say no, you are definitely doing too much.

Sign 6: If the person you are helping expects you to do more and more for them instead of being grateful for what you have done, you are helping too much.

Sign 7: If you continually cancel your plans because the one you are helping *needs* you to help them, you are probably doing too much for them.

Check Your Motives

Jesus gave His life sacrificially in order to help us, and being a blessing to other people is one of the things He has called us to do. Nothing makes us happier than helping and giving to others when we do it in a healthy way and for the right reasons.

Some people help others because it makes them feel good about themselves. They find their value in doing things for others even when what they are doing is harmful. My mother often did things for my brother that she should not have done. I often heard her say that she loved him so much she just couldn't say no. Actually, if we truly love people, we will say no if that is what will help them more than us saying yes. My mother thought she was helping my brother, but in reality she was hurting him.

I often watched him talk her out of her pain medication or into giving him money that she couldn't afford to give him. These so-called acts of kindness were simply feeding his addiction.

My mother had a poor self-image. She felt unloved and carried a lot of guilt because she had allowed my father to abuse me without taking action, and she masked her bad feelings by doing things for others. She helped because it made her feel good about herself, but in reality it was a cover-up for problems that she never dealt with.

An honest evaluation of our motives can be painful, but it can be one of the most freeing things that we ever do. The things we do can be completely without value if the reason we are doing them is wrong. Try asking God to show you why you do many of the things you do, especially the ones that seem to add stress to your life, and you may be surprised by what He reveals to you.

It does very little good to ask God to heal our wounded souls if we continue doing things that wound them over and over. God is in the healing business, and He delights in making us whole, but we need to cooperate with Him by doing everything He shows us that we need to do.

CHAPTER 21

The Blessings of a Healthy Soul

Bless the LORD, O my soul;
And all that is within me, bless His holy name!
Bless the LORD, O my soul,
And forget not all His benefits:
Who forgives all your iniquities,
Who heals all your diseases.

—Psalm 103:1–3 NKJV

When we embark on a long and perhaps uncomfortable journey, it helps us to ponder how wonderful it will be when we arrive at our destination. That is what I want us to do in this chapter.

When Jesus was facing the pain of being crucified and dying on the cross, the Bible says He endured the pain of it for the joy of the prize set before Him (Hebrews 12:2). I believe He was thinking of the resurrection and all the benefits it would offer to God's children. He was looking forward to returning to His rightful place at the right hand of His Father in heaven, where He was before He came to pay for our sins and offer us a new life in and through Him. Looking at the end from the beginning of a painful journey helps us not turn back when it is difficult. Since you may not have made your journey yet, you might not be aware of all the blessings that await you, so I hope to help you see what is waiting for you as you work with God toward having a healthy soul.

Is a wounded soul making you sick? Although all sicknesses are certainly not caused by the wounds in our souls, some of them are. Many people experience physical healing once their souls have been healed. A great deal of pain and disease is caused by the stress we carry that God never intended for us. His will is peace and joy, both of which foster good health, but the devil comes only to kill, steal, and destroy (John 10:10).

The apostle John prayed this:

> Beloved, I pray that you may prosper in every way and [that your body] may keep well, even as [I know] your soul keeps well and prospers (3 John 1:2).

In this Scripture we can see a connection between the healing of our soul and our body. The better it goes with our soul, the better it will go with our body.

For many years I was tired most of the time, didn't sleep well, and had daily headaches and other maladies. I can testify that the more my soul was healed and filled with peace and joy, the healthier I became. What is in us works its way out of us, so if we have pain in our souls, it often shows up in our bodies, and likewise, if we have peace in our souls, that will make its way into our bodies.

God teaches us that a merry heart works like a good medicine in our lives (Proverbs 17:22). The Scripture that I shared in the opening of this chapter is declaring that truth. When our soul can bless the Lord, we will experience deliverance from sin and its misery, and that can also include the healing of disease.

I doubt that we can properly ascertain the negative effects that abuse and mental and physical stress have on our health. I was already experiencing problems in my body by the time I was eighteen years old, and it is not surprising, considering the things I had gone through in my life by that time. I can testify that the more peace I have, the better I feel physically. Emotional stress drains us of the energy we need for daily life.

Perhaps you have never realized how much the condition of your soul affects your body, but they are definitely closely connected and affect one another greatly. Therefore, two of the things you can

> *Emotional stress drains us of the energy we need for daily life.*

look forward to as you continue your journey of healing are better health and more energy.

When Jesus was here on earth, He regularly healed people of their diseases, and He is still our Healer today. I believe that all healing comes from God. He may work through medical technology that He has given someone the wisdom to invent, or He may show us a change that we need to make in order to promote healing in our body, or He may work miraculously and do what no one else can do.

One of the most frequent prayer requests we receive in our office is for healing, and if you need physical healing, I want to encourage you to trust God to work in your body as well as in your soul. As you wait for your own healing, it is wise to reach out and help other people in need. I often find that although I cannot seem to solve my own problem, God does give me the ability to help someone else. As we help others, we are sowing seed that brings back a harvest of blessing in our own lives. Consider these three Scripture verses, and I think you will agree:

Blessed (happy, fortunate, to be envied) is he who considers the weak *and* the poor; the Lord will deliver him in the time of evil *and* trouble.

The Lord will protect him and keep him alive; he shall
be called blessed in the land; and You will not deliver him
to the will of his enemies.

The Lord will sustain, refresh, *and* strengthen him on
his bed of languishing; all his bed You [O Lord] will turn,
change, *and* transform in his illness (Psalm 41:1–3).

Confidence

Confidence is another side effect of a healed soul. God wants us
to be secure in His love for us and to believe that we can do whatever we need to do in life as long as we know who we are in Him.

I have strength for all things in Christ Who empowers me
[I am ready for anything and equal to anything through
Him Who infuses inner strength into me; I am self-
sufficient in Christ's sufficiency] (Philippians 4:13).

I never tire of meditating on this Scripture. Its promise is
amazing! We can be transformed from living with fear to living with a confident assurance that we are ready for anything in
life.

Our confidence should not be in what *we* can do but in what
Jesus can do through us. Knowing beyond any doubt that we
are loved unconditionally gives us courage to do things that
we might have otherwise been afraid of. We learn that even when
we make mistakes, God still loves us and is ready to help us.
Proverbs 24:16 tells us that a righteous man falls seven times and
rises again.

We may get knocked down in life, but if we are in Christ and
our soul is healthy, we will always get back up again. If you have

been lying in your pain and misery, watching from the sidelines as your life goes by, it is time for you to get up and get going again.

Confidence causes you to believe that *you can* instead of being afraid that you can't. No matter what others believe about you, it is what *you* believe that really matters. Henry David Thoreau said, "Public opinion is a weak tyrant compared with our own private opinion. What a man thinks of himself, that is which determines, or rather, indicates his fate."[25]

My father told me that I would never amount to anything, and as long as I believed him, he was right. But when God showed me that I could do all things through Christ, I learned that my father was wrong in his assessment of me. Lots of people are wrong in their assessment of you also. Don't let what people think of you or say about you determine your destiny.

> *It is what you believe about yourself that really matters.*

Confident people take chances and try things rather than fearfully assuming they will fail before they even try.

Amanda likes Bob, but she fears that he doesn't like her. She has suffered with insecurity and lacks confidence, and the story of her life has been that she never does what she really wants to do; instead, she shrinks back in fear. Amanda would like to walk up to Bob and talk to him. She would like to give him a compliment about some of the abilities she has seen him display, but she is afraid she will be rejected. Her fear of rejection causes her to be cold toward him, and he feels that she is unfriendly and difficult to get to know. Guess what happens? She ignores him, and he ignores her, and her fears become her reality. The cycle Amanda has experienced in her life continues, and she remains miserable.

It doesn't have to be that way. What could Amanda do to

change things? She could start by believing that God loves her, and because of that love, she can be confident. She also needs to change her self-talk. She has spent her life talking herself out of things, but she can change that and talk herself into things.

Science is discovering what God has been telling us all along: As a man thinks in his heart, so does he become (Proverbs 23:7).

University of Victoria psychologist Danu Anthony Stinson said, "Self-affirmation [contemplating personal values central to one's identity] seems to provide a psychological buffer for insecure people, allowing them to put aside social fears and anxieties and behave in more warm and inviting ways."[26]

Sadly, many women and girls derive most of their confidence by how they think they look, and they are determining that they do or don't look acceptable based on what society says. I believe that God made all things beautiful, and since He made us, we are all beautiful in our own way. Just because we don't look like someone else does not mean that we are not beautiful. You have probably heard that true beauty comes from the inside, and I believe that it is true. We focus way too much on our various body parts and not enough on the hidden person of the heart that God speaks about in His Word.

> Let not yours be the [merely] external adorning with [elaborate] interweaving and knotting of the hair, the wearing of jewelry, or changes of clothes;
>
> But let it be the inward adorning *and* beauty of the hidden person of the heart, with the incorruptible *and* unfading charm of a gentle and peaceful spirit, which [is not anxious or wrought up, but] is very precious in the sight of God (1 Peter 3:3–4).

I have changed my clothes three or more times before going out just to make sure that everything looks perfect. Although there is nothing wrong with looking nice, God has had to nudge me more than a few times to remember that my outfit for the day is not where my confidence needs to be.

An article commissioned by the Dove Self-Esteem Project revealed that there is a self-esteem crisis among girls in this country.[27]

- Sixty-two percent of all girls feel insecure and not sure of themselves.
- Fifty-seven percent of girls have a mother who criticizes their looks.
- Seventy-one percent of girls with low self-esteem feel their appearance does not measure up, including not feeling pretty enough, thin enough, or stylish or trendy enough.
- A girl's self-esteem is more strongly related to how she views her own body shape and body weight than how much she *actually* weighs.
- Sixty-one percent of teen girls with low self-esteem talk bad about themselves.
- Twenty-five percent of girls with low self-esteem say they engage in negative activities like overeating, cutting themselves, smoking, or drinking when they feel bad about themselves.

It is sad when girls and women spend their lives trying to find confidence in how they look, because no matter how good we look, there will always be someone who may look better according to the world's standards. Our confidence and beauty can be found in knowing Christ and becoming like Him.

Your Healing Affects Family and Friends

Just as the people in our lives are affected by our wounded souls, they are also affected by our healing. Keeping that in mind may help you press on toward victory on days when giving up is a temptation. I didn't intend for my wounds to hurt the people I love, but they did. I am very happy to say that my healing is now helping people.

Relationships are a large part of life, and we all want to enjoy good ones. Doing so becomes very difficult if we live with wounds, bruises, and pain in our inner life. We don't mean to hurt people, but we do. Because what is in us, comes out of us.

I am glad that I pressed through not only for myself but also for my family, friends, and all the people I touch in my daily life. Everywhere we go, we are affecting and touching people. At home, at school, at work, at church, or in our neighborhoods, we leave an impression on people. Whether I smile or don't smile at someone leaves an impression on them concerning what they think of me. If I am discouraged and depressed because of my pain and unhappiness, I am more likely not to smile or be friendly than if I am healed and happy. An act as simple as smiling at others can make them feel better about themselves. Our contact with others may be brief, but in some ways it may be lasting. People may not remember what we said to them, but they remember how we made them feel. The better you feel about yourself, the better you will make others feel about themselves.

> *The better you feel about yourself, the better you will make others feel about themselves.*

We have looked at three of the benefits of having a soul that is healed and healthy, but there are hundreds of others. I encourage you to look forward to all the good things that are waiting for you. God always rewards those who are diligent in seeking Him (Hebrews 11:6). Samuel Johnson said, "What we hope ever to do with ease, we must first do with diligence."[28] Doing things in a new way requires diligence, but I know from experience that what may feel almost impossible to you right now will one day be easy if you don't give up.

CHAPTER 22

The Painless Path

What comes easy won't last, what lasts won't come easy.
—Author unknown

If you saw the title of this chapter before you started reading the book, you may have turned to it first because most of us want a painless path. That is why someone can advertise a pill on television with the promise that taking one three times a day will cause fat to just melt off your body, and they sell millions of bottles of it. Our flesh always looks for the easy way out, but I don't want to give you false hope, so I will say openly that if your soul has been severely wounded through abuse, rejection, loss, abandonment, long-term illness, or any other thing, the journey toward healing won't be painless. But once you have healing, you can keep and enjoy it for the rest of your life.

Jesus told us that there is a narrow path in life and a broad one that we can walk. He advises us to take the narrow one, and the description of *narrow* tells us that it is the more difficult one to walk.

> Enter through the narrow gate; for wide is the gate and spacious *and* broad is the way that leads away to destruction, and many are those who are entering through it.

> But the gate is narrow (contracted by pressure) and the
> way is straitened *and* compressed that leads away to life,
> and few are those who find it (Matthew 7:13–14).

The broad path is the one that seems easier, although we ultimately find that it does not take us where we want to go. If we
stay on the broad path, which Jesus says leads to destruction, we
have plenty of room for our fleshly baggage, but on the narrow
path we don't. However, the narrow path leads to a life that is
worth living.

What do I mean by "fleshly baggage"? I mean that we continue
to behave according to our fleshly and carnal desires rather than
learning to follow the leadership and guidance of Jesus. We do
what we want to do instead of what He instructs us to do.

We are triune beings: we are a spirit, we have a soul, and we
live in a body. When the Bible refers to "the flesh," it is speaking
of the body and soul (mind, will, and emotions) combined. The
flesh is very different from the spirit. When we are born again
(receive Christ through faith), Jesus comes to live in us and our
spirit is filled with His Spirit, who seeks to guide us through life.
God wants us to choose what is right, but He never forces us to
do it.

Paul urged believers to "walk" in the spirit and not in the flesh.
The spirit is holy and good, but the flesh is filled with tendencies
toward evil. If, for example, a believer is walking in (or according
to) the flesh and someone offends her, she will follow her feelings
and choose to be angry and resentful, carrying a grudge and perhaps seeking revenge. On the other hand, if a believer is walking
in (or according to) the Spirit, she will resist the temptation to be
touchy and will choose to quickly forgive. She doesn't necessarily
make this choice because it is the easy one or the one she thinks

is fair or feels like doing, but she chooses it because it is the will of God. This is what it means to walk in the Spirit and not in the flesh.

When we make right choices according to the will of God, we are walking on the narrow path, not the broad path. When we make a decision to travel with Christ on the narrow road, we find that the path often becomes narrower the further we go, and we must, out of necessity, keep dropping various pieces of fleshly baggage in order to stay on the path. When people talk about others they know who have bad tempers, are terribly insecure, want to control others or are ruled by fear, I often hear them say: "They have a lot of baggage!"

The Holy Spirit shows us what baggage is to be left behind if we want to continue our journey with Him on the narrow path. A woman who recently attended one of my conferences said, "Wow, Joyce! God nailed me this morning, big time." What did she mean? She went on to tell me that she was doing a Bible study with a group of women and that her assignment for the week had been to listen to a teaching CD by the author of the Bible study. She said with a flushed face and great emotion, "God showed me in no uncertain terms that it was time for me to stop trying to control situations and let Him work in my life."

When she said that God "nailed her," she meant that He had definitely revealed to her that the baggage of trying to control situations and people had to go in order for her to progress any further on the path she was on. The type of understanding this woman was referring to is what the Bible calls revelation. It is something deeper than what we would normally call knowledge. It affects us deeply and leaves us with a certainty about what our next steps are to be.

A young man called me this morning, and when I saw his name

on my phone I was fairly certain I knew what he wanted. He had written me a hurtful email at a time when he was in great pain over the loss of his young wife to cancer. We had helped him a great deal, but in the end he felt that we had failed and abandoned him. The email he sent was totally out of character for him, and I was not only hurt but also surprised. I had been praying for a few months that he would apologize, and I can honestly say that I wanted it more for him than I even did for myself. I knew that he needed to repent and that if he didn't, sooner or later his actions would become a hindrance to him.

When I answered the phone, he promptly told me that he was very sorry for the email he had sent and that he realized he was just looking for somewhere to place blame, hoping it would relieve his own suffering. We talked for a while, and he shared with me that he had been under a lot of stress trying to do certain things and felt a blockage or a hindrance to God's anointing (power and presence), and that as he prayed, asking God what was wrong, it was revealed to him that he needed to repent for the email he had sent and the attitude he had at the time he sent it.

I was glad to receive the apology because I didn't want any strife in our relationship, but I was also thrilled for him because I knew he had taken action that would now release him to move forward.

When we truly want to hear from God, He will speak to us, but we may not always like what we hear. We usually want something that is easy to do, but God wants to give us grace (ease) to do very dif- ficult things. Doing the right thing

> *Doing the right thing when everything about it feels wrong is the pathway to progress.*

when everything about it feels wrong is the pathway to progress.

Recently, I was working out with my trainer and it seemed that everything I was doing that day was hard. All the weights seemed heavier than normal, and I just wanted to get the workout over with. I said, "This is really hard today." He responded, "If it is easy, then you aren't making much progress." That wasn't what I wanted to hear, but the thought that I was making progress did make the discomfort easier to bear.

Is Anything Really Free?

When we hear the word *free* we get excited. You should see how people react in our conferences if we take a stack of books and teaching CDs and tell them we are going to give them to a few people for free. Those who are normally quite reserved in how they present themselves often lose all decorum and rush toward the front of the auditorium, hoping to be one of the people selected to get a free gift.

If we offer a free booklet on our television program for anyone who calls and asks for it, our calls that day can increase tenfold. We get excited about getting something that we think is free, but nothing is ever really free. Even if we get it for free, it cost someone else somewhere along the way before it got to us. The Bible says that it is by *free* grace that we are saved and delivered from our sins (Ephesians 2:8). Our salvation is free to us, but it cost Jesus His life.

The painless path is not the best one to look for, because even if you found one, you probably wouldn't end up where you wanted to go. I deeply appreciate the life I have now because it was painful to acquire. It required effort, diligence, and willingness to keep going when everything in me wanted to quit. My healing from abuse and the wounds that resulted was not a quick thing. It took a lot longer than I thought it would and was harder than

I expected it would be, but I don't have words suitable to tell you how wonderful and enjoyable it is.

I think one can only truly appreciate freedom from bondage when they have suffered deeply to become free. We usually take better care of and appreciate more the things that we have that cost us the most. Your freedom from your wounded soul may require effort on your part, but you will value it more than you can imagine.

I can't imagine what my life would have been like had I not chosen the narrow path. I doubt that anyone could have put up with me for very long, so I would have probably been married more times than Zsa Zsa Gabor—and she was married nine times. Any children I had would not have liked me very much, if at all. I would have no real friends and would have lived a lonely, desperate life. Dave often says that he feels like he has been married to twenty different women, because each time God changed me, he got a better version of me. On the narrow path you keep getting better, but on the broad path you either remain the same or you may get worse.

Stay on the narrow path, even when it seems difficult. The Holy Spirit will lead you at a pace that is right for you, and along the way you can appreciate and celebrate each little victory that you have. Don't make the mistake of only looking at how far you still have to go and everything you think is wrong with you. All that matters to God is that you are willing to make the journey and you're making a little more progress each day.

Quick Fixes

We love it when things that are broken get fixed quickly, but with God there are not a lot of quick fixes. We usually think that God moves at a very slow pace, but He does so because He is more concerned with quality and depth than He is with quick fixes.

Our prayer is often "Lord, please make me patient and do it right now!" The Bible says that we must "let endurance and steadfastness and patience have full play and do a thorough work" so that we may be perfect and entire, lacking in nothing (James 1:4). God has an end goal in mind, and He is willing to do anything necessary and take any amount of time required for us to reach His goal.

A mushroom can grow overnight, but a large oak or a giant sequoia takes a long time. The question is, do we want to be a mushroom or a giant tree of righteousness that never ceases bearing good fruit (Jeremiah 17:8)? Our Lord Jesus spent thirty years preparing for a three-year ministry, but the power of those three years will endure forever. Joseph prepared thirteen years for his role as prime minister of Egypt, and then God used him to save many people from starvation during famine.

Diamonds are among some of the most valued jewels on earth, and they are formed very slowly, at high temperatures under great pressure from being buried in the depths of the earth. Geodes are rocks that have an ugly exterior but are beautiful on the inside because the inner lining is coated with crystals of various colors.

We can use the examples of diamonds and geodes as we think about ourselves. As we begin our journey with God toward healing and wholeness, our behavior may be quite unattractive, but inside of us (in our spirit), where the Holy Spirit lives, exists great beauty and capacity for good. It takes time for us to go through the transformation process so that the work God has done on the inside of us is revealed in our outer lives. And we will experience heat and pressure in the journey to break off the outer hull so what is inside can be poured out. But when the work is done, we are in awe of the magnificent change God has created in us.

This quote from *Othello,* by William Shakespeare, sums up a point I'm making here very well:

How poor are they that have not patience! What wound
did ever heal but by degrees?[29]

Our wounds heal by degrees. It takes time and persistence in
doing the right thing to properly care for the wound. If someone has
a wound and goes to the doctor, the doctor may prescribe a medi-
cated ointment with instructions to keep the wound clean, apply
the ointment twice daily, and keep it bandaged. Also, the prescription for the ointment may offer refills if needed. We don't expect to
come home and apply the ointment once and be totally healed. We
know that it will be a process and that we will need to be diligent.

The principle is the same with emotional wounds as with
physical ones. We must be patient and continue doing the things
that God leads us to do, and gradually our wounds will heal. The
practice of patience may be bitter, but its fruit is sweet.

Pick Your Pain

Most of us would prefer life without any pain, but when it comes
to making a choice to let God heal
our wounds or stay the way we are,
we have to pick our pain. Do you
want the temporary pain of progress or the eternal pain of staying
the same?

> Do you want the temporary pain
> of progress or the eternal pain of
> staying the same?

I find that pain of any kind is much easier to endure if I
know that it is leading to something good. For example, I made
the choice to let go of anger and forgive those who had hurt me
because I knew the blessing would be to have peace and be in
God's will. I sometimes give away things I would love to keep for
myself because I know that giving produces joy and brings a great

harvest in my life. If you take time to think about it, we all make many decisions each day that require us to give up one thing we want in order to have another thing that we want even more.

I am sure you frequently make a decision that is not easy or comfortable at the moment because you realize the joy that lies on the other side of it. Making the decision to let God open all the wounds in your soul and heal them so you can enjoy the life Jesus died to give you may not be easy, but living with the wounds is much more difficult.

I saw a movie about a woman who had been deceived by a man she loved, and each time she saw him or even heard his name she felt bitter and angry. He asked her to forgive him, but she felt that she could not do it. A pastor was talking with her about the situation, and he said, "If you have a really bad toothache and your only choice is to have it pulled, there is no point in putting it off because you dread the pain that will be involved."

This movie was set in the 1800s, before dentists had numbing medicines, so I would imagine that having a tooth pulled would have been quite painful. Yet, the pastor reminded her that although having the tooth pulled would hurt for a short while, keeping the tooth meant it would never stop hurting. He said, "If you forgive the man who hurt you, it will be like pulling a painful tooth. You do it and get it over with so you can stop hurting."

The narrow path is not without pain, but on that road you always have Jesus with you. It was the path He chose to walk, and the one He urges us to choose. You have a great victory waiting for you, and each step you take in the right direction brings you a little closer to it. I ask you to open every room in your heart to God and trust that He will fill it with light, love, and joy.

CHAPTER 23

The Great Exchange

The Spirit of the Sovereign LORD is on me,
because the LORD has anointed me
to proclaim good news to the poor.
He has sent me to bind up the brokenhearted,
to proclaim freedom for the captives
and release from darkness for the prisoners,
to proclaim the year of the LORD's favor
and the day of vengeance of our God,
to comfort all who mourn,
and provide for those who grieve in Zion—
to bestow on them a crown of beauty
instead of ashes,
the oil of joy
instead of mourning,
and a garment of praise
instead of a spirit of despair.
They will be called oaks of righteousness,
a planting of the LORD
for the display of his splendor.

                    —Isaiah 61:1–3 NIV

What if you knew there was a store in your city where you could take anything worn-out, ineffective, ruined, old, or no longer working and exchange it for a brand-new one at no cost? If such a store existed, I doubt that you would waste any time in beginning to exchange many things—I know I wouldn't. The only requirement at this store is that you must turn in the old item that is ruined before you can receive the new one.

Jesus invites us to live an exchanged life. On any day, we can exchange a bad attitude for a good one, our sins for forgiveness, our failures for mercy, hopelessness for hope, and thousands of other good things. But we don't get the new one until we turn in the old one.

If we are willing to give ourselves—everything we are and have—to Jesus, He will give us everything He has and is (John 16:15). What He offers is immeasurably better than what we give up. Just think of it: Everything the Father has is ours, and all we need to do is give up our old ideas and ways in order to experience it in every area of our lives.

Why are we so reluctant to let go of the old? I think because there is no mystery in old things—we may not like them, but at least they are not a surprise to us. The thought of walking away from what we have and not knowing what we are walking toward is frightening, and because of that, many people refuse to do it. They live an inferior, painful, unproductive life that they do not enjoy when they could exchange it for a new one.

God's exchange store is always open, and He's always available to meet with you. The sad thing is most people don't know that it even exists, and if they do, they have difficulty believing that its claims are true.

Beauty for Ashes

A man I recently met said, "Joyce, I was abused in my childhood like you were. At that point I stopped living and started surviving, and that is all I did until I heard you say that God wanted to give me beauty for ashes. After that my life changed, and I will never be the same again."

This man had been a Christian for quite a while, and he went to church with his pain and then took it home with him. He didn't know about the great exchange.

Isaiah 61:1–3 was certainly life-changing for me, as well as for the man I met, and I pray it will be for you also. God wants to give you a beautiful soul and a beautiful life, and He will take the ashes of your past and make something beautiful and new out of them. God is able to work out anything and everything for our good if we will let Him (Romans 8:28). The first step is to believe in Jesus, and to also believe that each of His promises are for you... that they can become a reality in your life as you take the steps of faith that He directs you to take.

Perhaps your identity has become *I'm wounded from my past*, but it can be *I'm a new creature in Christ*. The promise of receiving beauty for ashes gives us hope, and it motivates us to move forward instead of staying parked at the point of our pain and merely surviving when we could be truly living and enjoying life.

The one thing we must do is give up our ashes, and that means we stop thinking and talking about the past unless we really need to for some reason. It also means we believe that with God's help, our past can become a distant memory. When I think or talk now about my childhood, it often seems that I am thinking or talking about someone that I once knew a long, long time ago.

Jesus has opened the prison doors, and all we need to do is walk out and start our new life with Him. He came to set captives free and to help those who have been afflicted and are brokenhearted. He not only opens the prison doors, according to Isaiah, but He opens our eyes. Even if the doors to the prison we live in have been opened, we won't walk out unless we see

that they are open, and God's Word

Jesus has opened the prison doors, and all we need to do is walk out with Him.

shows us that they are. It makes me very sad when I think about how many believers in Christ live with wounded souls because they have not been told that Jesus has opened the prison doors and they can be free.

Jesus wants to comfort those who mourn, who are sad and grieving. He came to announce the good news that now is the time for God's favor. Perhaps you have always felt like the tail end of everything in life. Perhaps you were the one who was never picked to be on the team or who never received an award when they were being given out. You may have felt last in your life, but it is a new day—the day of the favor of God!

When God gives us favor it means that He opens doors of opportunity for us that only He can open and causes us to be the head and not the tail, above and not beneath as He promised (Deuteronomy 28:13). Can you imagine the joy of living with God's favor? We may think that having the favor of our supervisor at work would be wonderful, but that pales in comparison to having God's favor. All true promotion comes from God, and He can put you in places and give you positions of honor that will amaze you.

Joy Instead of Mourning

People who have been deeply wounded often live with a grieving or a mourning spirit. They have a sadness about them that's hard to explain. They may have lived with it for so long that they don't even recognize it for what it is. I always felt that I was burdened in some way or that a type of heaviness existed in my soul until I found out that I could exchange that feeling for joy and praise.

Making the exchange begins with a decision to believe that with God all things are possible, and as we remain steadfast and patient, the bad feelings will give way to joyous ones. The joy replaces the heavy, burdened, and failing spirit we have suffered with.

You don't have to keep something that isn't working—you can exchange it. If our cell phone isn't working, it doesn't take us long to go to the store and exchange it or have it repaired, but oddly we put up with lives that aren't working. However, that doesn't need to be the case any longer, because now you know that Jesus is waiting to exchange it. I bought a pair of shoes recently, and they squeak when I walk. I was in the store where I purchased them and told the salesman who was waiting on me about the shoes, and he said, "Bring them back and we will exchange them—no questions asked."

> You don't have to keep something that isn't working.

I shop a lot in that particular store, and one of the major reasons is because of their exchange policy. I have confidence that if I get anything that is not working for me, I can take it back and they will replace it. If having a store like that excites us, then how excited should we be to find out that God has a store like that, too?

God's Righteousness for Ours

We will never be able to do enough right things on our own to be pleasing to God. Isaiah said that our righteousness is like filthy rags or a polluted garment (Isaiah 64:6). God is perfect, and in order for our righteousness to be acceptable to God as an offering for our sins, it would have to be perfect; that is not possible for flawed and weak humans like us. But don't despair—we can exchange our imperfect righteousness for God's perfect righteousness because of what Jesus has done for us.

> For our sake He made Christ [virtually] to be sin Who knew no sin, so that in *and* through Him we might become [endued with, viewed as being in, and examples of] the righteousness of God [what we ought to be, approved and acceptable and in right relationship with Him, by His goodness] (2 Corinthians 5:21).

If you rushed past this Scripture, as we often do when reading books, I ask you to go back and read it slowly and think about the beauty of what is being said. What a glorious exchange! It becomes ours through believing it.

Most of my life I had the sense that something was wrong with me, though I never knew definitely what it was. I had a recording that played endlessly in my head that said, *What is wrong with me? What is wrong with me?* It started in my childhood when I was being abused and felt certain that something must be wrong with me for my father to want to do the despicable things that he was doing to me. I felt certain it wasn't happening to other little girls, although I have since learned how tragically common it is. The longer the abuse continued, the more deeply flawed I felt.

Imagine my joy when I learned that God, because of His goodness, viewed me as being right. It did take a long time for all the feelings of being wrong to completely fade away, but little by little they did, and it is wonderful to live without guilt and shame and to know and believe that God approves of me. The same thing is available to anyone who needs it and is willing to believe God and let go of the old. It helped me to meditate on and confess this Scripture, and others like it, about being made right with God. It helped renew my mind to God's truth rather than the lies of Satan I had believed most of my life. Gradually, the old recording in my mind was replaced with a new one.

Under the Old Covenant law that the Israelites lived with, in order to be forgiven of sin, the sinner brought an animal sacrifice to the altar of God, and either he or the priest laid his hands on the head of the animal and confessed his sin and guilt. They believed the sin was being put on the animal that was then put to death in place of the sinner who deserved death.

Jesus is called "the Lamb of God, Who takes away the sin of the world" (John 1:29). When John made that announcement, the Jews knew what he meant because they often used a lamb for their sacrifices. Jesus offers us the great exchange—He takes our sin and we receive His forgiveness. Under the Old Covenant sin was covered, but Jesus removes our sin as far as the east is from the west.

> As far as the east is from the west, so far has He removed our transgressions from us (Psalm 103:12).
>
> For I will be merciful *and* gracious toward their sins and I will remember their deeds of unrighteousness no more (Hebrews 8:12).
>
> And their sins and their lawbreaking I will remember no more. Now where there is absolute remission (forgiveness and cancellation of the penalty) of these [sins and lawbreaking], there is no longer any offering made to atone for sin (Hebrews 10:17–18).

Sin is no longer just covered up, always vaguely reminding you of what you have done and leaving you feeling guilty; it is completely removed! Let Jesus take your sin and guilt and exchange it for His forgiveness and right standing with God.

Mercy for Failures

We can exchange our failures for God's mercy. Paul taught that we should go boldly to the throne of God's grace and receive mercy for our failures (Hebrews 4:16). Mercy is God giving us what we do not deserve. He helps us, answers our prayers, provides for us, and loves us unconditionally, and we don't deserve any of it. But because of His great mercy, it is ours as a gift from Him.

The list of things we can exchange is far too long for me to share all of them in this book, but there is another book that contains them all, and that is the Bible. I want to encourage you to read and study it so you can discover everything God has for you—not as a religious obligation or because you feel it is your duty as a Christian. The Bible is simply the greatest book on the earth, and it is filled with promises that are astounding…and they are all yours in Christ!

AFTERWORD

My prayer is that this book will help millions of people recover from the wounds in their soul and live a life of healing and wholeness. If you have not received Jesus as your Savior and Lord, I urge you to pray the prayer at the end of this book and get started right away with your new life. Know that you can never visit the exchange store too often. Go several times every day if you need to. Never forget that you are precious and dearly loved, and that not only has Jesus gone before us into heaven to prepare a place for us where we will live with Him for eternity, He has also arranged for us to live a fulfilling and abundant life during our journey here on earth. It won't be one without challenge and difficulty, but with Him living in us, we can live in victory. You are more than a conqueror through Christ, who loves you!

Voting Rights

When women received the ability to vote around the world:
1893 New Zealand
1902 Australia[1]
1906 Finland
1913 Norway
1915 Denmark
1917 Canada[2]
1918 Austria, Germany, Poland, Russia
1919 Netherlands
1920 United States
1921 Sweden
1928 Britain, Ireland
1931 Spain
1934 Turkey
1944 France
1945 Italy
1947 Argentina, Japan, Mexico, Pakistan
1949 China
1950 India
1954 Colombia
1957 Malaysia, Zimbabwe

1962 Algeria

1963 Iran, Morocco

1964 Libya

1967 Ecuador

1971 Switzerland

1972 Bangladesh

1976 Portugal

1989 Namibia

1994 South Africa

2005 Kuwait

2006 United Arab Emirates

2011 Saudi Arabia[3]

1. Australian women, with the exception of aboriginal women, won the vote in 1902. Aborigines, male and female, did not have the right to vote until 1962.

2. Canadian women, with the exception of Canadian Indian women, won the vote in 1917. Canadian Indians, male and female, did not win the vote until 1960. Source: *New York Times*, May 22, 2005.

3. King Abdullah issued a decree in 2011 ordering that women be allowed to stand as candidates and vote in municipal elections, but their first opportunity did not come until December 2015, almost a year after the king's death in January 2015.

Source: http://www.infoplease.com/ipa/A0931343.html.

Pay Inequality

In the US, the median annual pay for a woman who holds a full-time, year-round job is $40,742 while the median annual pay for a man who holds a full-time, year-round job is $51,212. This means that, overall, women in the United States are paid 80 cents for every dollar paid to men, amounting to an annual gender wage gap of $10,470.

Source: US Census Bureau. (2016). *Current Population Survey, Annual Social and Economic (ASEC) Supplement: Table PINC-05: Work Experience in 2015—People 15 Years Old and Over by Total Money Earnings in 2015, Age, Race, Hispanic Origin, Sex, and Disability Status.* Retrieved October 12, 2016, from http://www.census.gov/data/tables/time-series/demo/income-poverty/cps-pinc/pinc-05.html (unpublished calculation based on the median annual pay for all women and men who worked full time, year-round in 2015).

As of January 2017, women currently hold 27 (5.4 percent) of CEO positions at those S&P 500 companies.

Source: http://www.catalyst.org/knowledge/women-ceos-sp -500.

Percentage of pay gap around the world (the percentage is how much more men make than women around the world):

Rank	Country	% Pay Gap
1	Korea	37.5
2	Russia	32.1
3	Estonia	27.9
4	Japan	27.4
5	Cyprus	25.1
6	India	24.81
7	Ukraine	22.2
8	Germany	20.8
9	Israel	20.7
10	Austria	19.2
11	Canada	19.2
12	Finland	18.9
13	Switzerland	18.5
14	United Kingdom	18.2

15	Czech Republic	18.1
16	United States	17.8
17	China	17.5
18	Luxembourg	17.3
19	Netherlands	16.7
20	Latvia	16.5

Source: http://www.movehub.com/blog/global-gender-pay-gap -map.

Property Rights

Mississippi allowed women to own property in their own names in 1839. It was the first state to do so. In 1844, married women in Maine became the first in the US to win the right to "separate economy" (if a woman had a job and made money, she could fully control the appropriation of those funds and wouldn't have to first get permission, legally, from her husband).

Source: https://en.wikipedia.org/wiki/Timeline_of_women's _legal_rights_(other_than_voting).

Education

A girl with an extra year of education can earn 20 percent more as an adult.

Source: abcnews.go.com (2013).

Worldwide, there are still 31 million girls of primary school age out of school. Of these, 17 million are expected never to enter school. There are 4 million fewer boys than girls out of school. Three countries have over 1 million girls not in school: in Nigeria, there are almost 5.5 million; in Pakistan, over 3 million; and in Ethiopia, over 1 million girls out of school (as of 2013).

Source: United Nations Educational, Scientific and Cultural Organization, http://en.unesco.org/gem-report/sites/gem-report/files/girls-factsheet-en.pdf.

Educated women are less likely to die in childbirth: If all mothers completed primary education, maternal deaths would be reduced by two-thirds, saving 98,000 lives. In Sub-Saharan Africa, if all women completed primary education, maternal deaths would be reduced by 70 percent, saving almost 50,000 lives.

Source: United Nations Educational, Scientific and Cultural Organization, http://en.unesco.org/gem-report/sites/gem-report/files/girls-factsheet-en.pdf (note: multiple tabs).

Gendercide

After birth, baby girls are more often neglected to death than actively killed, but families still continue to drown, smother, strangle, and abandon baby girls. Currently, we lose about 2 million baby girls per year to gendercide.

Source: Valarie M. Hudson and Andrea M. den Boer, *Bare Branches: The Security Implications of Asia's Surplus Male Population* (Cambridge, MA: MIT Press, 2005), 112–113, 157. See also Mara Hvistendahl, *Unnatural Selection: Choosing*

Boys over Girls, and the Consequences of a World Full of Men
(New York: Public Affairs, 2011).

Where does gendercide occur?
- East Asia: China, Vietnam, Singapore, and Taiwan
- South Asia: India, Bangladesh, Nepal, Pakistan, and Afghanistan
- West Asia: Turkey, Syria, Iran, Azerbaijan, Armenia, and Georgia
- Eastern Europe: Albania, Romania, Montenegro, Kosovo, and Macedonia
- North Africa: Egypt, Tunisia, and Algeria
- Sub-Saharan Africa: most countries
- Asian American communities within the US and Canada

Source: Klasen and Wink, *Missing Women: A Review of the Debates and an Analysis of Recent Trends*, 2002, available at SSRN: https://ssrn.com/abstract=321861, p. 19. For data concerning the United States, see Douglas Almond and Lena Edlund, "Son-Biased Sex Ration in the 2000 United States Census," *Proceedings of the National Academy of Sciences* 105, no. 15 (April 15, 2008): 5681–5682.

Female Genital Mutilation

Female genital mutilation (FGM) includes procedures that intentionally alter or cause injury to the female genital organs for nonmedical reasons. The procedure has no health benefits for girls and women. Procedures can cause severe bleeding and problems urinating, and later cysts, infections, as well as complications in childbirth and increased risk of newborn deaths. More than 200 million girls and women alive today have been cut in thirty countries in Africa, the Middle East, and Asia, where FGM is concentrated. FGM is mostly carried out on young girls between infancy and age fifteen. FGM is a violation of the human rights of girls and women.

Source: J. Simister, "Domestic Violence and Female Genital Mutilation in Kenya: Effects of Ethnicity and Education," *Journal of Family Violence* 25, no. 3 (2010): 247–257.

About 100–140 million girls and women worldwide are living with the consequences of FGM, approximately 3.3 million girls are at risk of FGM each year, and in the twenty-eight countries for which national prevalence data exist (twenty-seven in Africa plus Yemen), more than 101 million girls ten years old and older are living with the effects of FGM.

Source: P. S. Yoder, S. Wang, and R. E. B. Johansen, "Female Genital Mutilation/Cutting in African Countries: Estimates of Numbers from National Surveys," unpublished paper.

Immediate and long-term health consequences of female genital mutilation:
- Severe pain
- Shock
- Hemorrhage (excessive bleeding)
- Sepsis
- Difficulty in passing urine
- Infections
- Death
- Psychological consequences

- Unintended labia fusion
- Need for surgery
- Urinary and menstrual problems
- Painful sexual intercourse and poor quality of sexual life
- Infertility
- Chronic pain
- Infections (e.g., cysts, abscesses, and genital ulcers, chronic pelvic infections, urinary tract infections)

Source: WHO Study Group on Female Genital Mutilation and Obstetric Outcome, "Female Genital Mutilation and Obstetric Outcome: WHO Collaborative Prospective Study in Six African Countries," *Lancet* 367, no. 9525 (2006):1835–1841; R. Berg, E. Denison, and A. Fretheim, *Psychological, Social, and Sexual Consequences of Female Genital Mutilation/Cutting (FGM/C): A Systematic Review of Quantitative Studies* (Oslo: Nasjonalt Kunnskapssenter for Helsetjenesten, 2010).

Violence and Abuse against Women

Women who have been physically or sexually abused by their partners are more than twice as likely to have an abortion, almost twice as likely to experience depression, and in some regions 1.5 times more likely to acquire HIV as compared to women who have not experienced partner violence.

Source: World Health Organization, Department of Reproductive Health and Research, London School of Hygiene and Tropical Medicine, South African Medical Research Council, *Global and Regional Estimates of Violence against Women: Prevalence and Health Effects of Intimate Partner Violence and*

Non-Partner Sexual Violence, 2013, p. 2. For individual country information, see United Nations Department of Economic and Social Affairs, *The World's Women 2015, Trends and Statistics*, chapter 6, "Violence against Women," 2015.

One in five women on US college campuses have experienced sexual assault.

Source: https://www.ncjrs.gov/pdffiles1/nij/grants/221153.pdf.

Most research concludes that girls and women are at substantially higher risk of being sexually assaulted than males.

Source: Aphrodite Matsakis, *When the Bough Breaks* (Oakland, CA: New Harbinger Publications, 1991).

A study of all state prisoners serving time for violent crime in 1991 revealed that of all those convicted for rape or sexual assault, two-thirds victimized children and three out of four of their victims were young girls.

Source: Lawrence Greenfeld, *Child Victimizers: Violent Offenders and Their Victims: Executive Summary* (Washington, DC: Bureau of Justice Statistics and the Office of Juvenile Justice and Delinquency Prevention, US Department of Justice, 1996).

Incest

Research indicates that 46 percent of children who are raped are victims of family members.

Source: Patrick Langan and Caroline Harlow, *Child Rape Victims, 1992* (Washington, DC: Bureau of Justice Statistics, US Department of Justice, 1994).

One of the nation's leading researchers on child sexual abuse, David Finkelhor, estimates that 1 million Americans are victims of father-daughter incest, and 16,000 new cases occur annually.

Source: David Finkelhor, *The Dark Side of Families: Current Family Violence Research* (Newbury Park, CA: Sage Publications, 1983).

- Incest can have serious long-term effects on its victims. One study concluded that among the survivors of incest who were victimized by their mothers, 60 percent of the women had eating disorders.

Source: National Center for Victims of Crime and Crime Victims Research and Treatment Center, *Rape in America: A Report to the Nation* (Arlington, VA: National Center for Victims of Crime and Crime Victims Research and Treatment Center, 1992); Heidi Vanderbilt, Heidi, "Incest: A Chilling Report," *Lears* (February 1992): 49–77.

Human Trafficking

Ludwig "Tarzan" Fainberg, a convicted trafficker, said, "You can buy a woman for $10,000 and make your money back in a week if she is pretty and young. Then everything else is profit."

Source: E. Benjamin Skinner, *A Crime So Monstrous: Face-to-Face with Modern-Day Slavery* (New York: Free Press, 2008).

A human trafficker can earn twenty times what he or she paid for a girl. Provided the girl was not physically brutalized to the point of ruining her beauty, the pimp could sell her again for a greater price because he had trained her and broken her spirit, which saves future buyers the hassle. A 2003 study in the Netherlands found that, on average, a single sex slave earned her pimp at least $250,000 a year.

Source: E. Benjamin Skinner, *A Crime So Monstrous: Face-to-Face with Modern-Day Slavery* (New York: Free Press, 2008).

According to the US State Department, 600,000 to 800,000 people are trafficked across international borders every year, of which 80 percent are female and half are children.

Source: https://www.dosomething.org/us/facts/11-facts-about -human-trafficking.

The National Human Trafficking Hotline receives more calls from Texas than any other state in the US. Fifteen percent of those calls are from the Dallas–Fort Worth area.

Source: https://www.dosomething.org/us/facts/11-facts-about -human-trafficking.

Human trafficking is the third largest international crime industry (behind illegal drugs and arms trafficking). It reportedly generates a profit of $32 billion every year. Of that number, $15.5 billion is made in industrialized countries.

Source: https://www.dosomething.org/us/facts/11-facts-about -human-trafficking.

Researchers note that sex trafficking plays a major role in the spread of HIV.

Source: Anthony M. Destefano, *The War on Human Trafficking* (Piscataway, NJ: Rutgers University Press, 2007).

Over 71 percent of trafficked children show suicidal tendencies.

Source: E. Benjamin Skinner, *A Crime So Monstrous: Face-to-Face with Modern-Day Slavery* (New York: Free Press, 2008).

According to the FBI, a large human trafficking organization in California in 2008 not only physically threatened and beat girls as young as twelve to work as prostitutes, they also regularly threatened them with witchcraft.

Source: FBI, "International Human Trafficking," November 13, 2009.   https://www.fbi.gov/audio-repository/news-podcasts-inside-international-human-trafficking.mp3/view.

APPENDIX II:
WHO YOU ARE IN CHRIST JESUS

I have received the spirit of wisdom and revelation in the knowledge of Jesus, the eyes of my understanding being enlightened (Ephesians 1:17–18).

I have received the power of the Holy Spirit to lay hands on the sick and see them recover, to cast out demons, to speak with new tongues. I have power over all the power of the enemy, and nothing shall by any means harm me (Mark 16:17–18; Luke 10:17–19).

I have put off the old man and have put on the new man, which is renewed in the knowledge after the image of Him, who created me (Colossians 3:9–10).

I have given, and it is given to me; good measure, pressed down, shaken together, and running over, men give into my bosom (Luke 6:38).

I have no lack for my God supplies all of my need according to His riches in glory by Christ Jesus (Philippians 4:19).

I can quench all the fiery darts of the wicked one with my shield of faith (Ephesians 6:16).

I can do all things through Christ Jesus (Philippians 4:13).

I show forth the praises of God, who has called me out of darkness into His marvelous light (1 Peter 2:9).

I am God's child, for I am born again of the incorruptible seed of the Word of God, which lives and abides forever (1 Peter 1:23).

I am God's workmanship, created in Christ unto good works (Ephesians 2:10).

I am a new creature in Christ (2 Corinthians 5:17).

I am a spirit being alive to God (Romans 6:11; Thessalonians 5:23).

I am a believer, and the light of the gospel shines in my mind (2 Corinthians 4:4).

I am a doer of the Word and blessed in my actions (James 1:22, 25).

I am a joint-heir with Christ (Romans 8:17).

I am more than a conqueror through Him, who loves me (Romans 8:37).

I am an overcomer by the blood of the Lamb and the word of my testimony (Revelation 12:11).

I am a partaker of His divine nature (2 Peter 1:3–4).

I am an ambassador for Christ (2 Corinthians 5:20).

I am part of a chosen generation, a royal priesthood, a holy nation, a purchased people (1 Peter 2:9).

I am the righteousness of God in Jesus Christ (2 Corinthians 5:21).

I am the temple of the Holy Spirit; I am not my own (1 Corinthians 6:19).

I am the head and not the tail; I am above only and not beneath (Deuteronomy 28:13).

I am the light of the world (Matthew 5:14).

I am His elect, full of mercy, kindness, humility, and long suffering (Romans 8:33; Colossians 3:12).

I am forgiven of all my sins and washed in the Blood (Ephesians 1:7).

I am delivered from the power of darkness and translated into God's kingdom (Colossians 1:13).

I am redeemed from the curse of sin, sickness, and poverty (Deuteronomy 28:15–68; Galatians 3:13).

I am firmly rooted, built up, established in my faith, and overflowing with gratitude (Colossians 2:7).

I am called of God to be the voice of His praise (Psalm 66:8; 2 Timothy 1:9).

I am healed by the stripes of Jesus (Isaiah 53:5; 1 Peter 2:24).

I am raised up with Christ and seated in heavenly places (Ephesians 2:6; Colossians 2:12).

I am greatly loved by God (Romans 1:7; Ephesians 2:4; Colossians 3:12; 1 Thessalonians 1:4).

I am strengthened with all might according to His glorious power (Colossians 1:11).

ENDNOTES

1 http://www.history.com/topics/womens-history/19th-amendment.
2 US Census Bureau. (2016). *Current Population Survey, Annual Social and Economic (ASEC) Supplement: Table PINC-01. Selected Characteristics of People 15 Years and Over, by Total Money Income in 2015, Work Experience in 2015, Race, Hispanic Origin, and Sex.* Retrieved 12 October 2016, from http://www.census.gov/data/tables/time-series/demo/income-poverty/cps-pinc/pinc-01.html (unpublished calculation based on the mean annual pay for all women and men who worked full-time, year-round in 2015, multiplied by the total number of women working full-time, year-round in 2015).
3 abcnews.go.com (2013).
4 United Nations Educational, Scientific and Cultural Organization, http://en.unesco.org/gem-report/sites/gem-report/files/girls-factsheet-en.pdf.
5 United Nations Educational, Scientific and Cultural Organization, http://en.unesco.org/gem-report/sites/gem-report/files/girls-factsheet-en.pdf (note: multiple tabs).
6 Gendercide Awareness Project, Gendap.org.
7 Valarie M. Hudson and Andrea M. den Boer, *Bare Branches: The Security Implications of Asia's Surplus Male Population* (Cambridge, MA: MIT Press, 2005), 109–113, 171–172. See also Mara Hvistendahl, *Unnatural Selection: Choosing Boys over Girls, and the Consequences of a World Full of Men* (New York: Public Affairs, 2011).
8 World Health Organization, Department of Reproductive Health and Research, London School of Hygiene and Tropical Medicine,

South African Medical Research Council, *Global and Regional Estimates of Violence against Women: Prevalence and Health Effects of Intimate Partner Violence and Non-Partner Sexual Violence*, 2013, p. 2. For individual country information, see United Nations Department of Economic and Social Affairs, *The World's Women 2015, Trends and Statistics*, Chapter 6, "Violence against Women," 2015.

9 UNODC, *Global Report on Trafficking in Persons*, 2014, pp. 5, 11.

10 International Labour Organization, *Minimum Estimate of Forced Labour in the World* (April 2005), p. 6.

11 https://www.dosomething.org/us/facts/11-facts-about-human -trafficking.

12 Skinner, E. Benjamin, *A Crime So Monstrous: Face-to-Face with Modern-Day Slavery* (New York: Free Press, 2008).

13 https://www.goodreads.com/quotes/230438-in-a-futile-attempt-to -erase-our-past-we-deprive.

14 https://www.goodreads.com/quotes/255850-of-one-thing-i-am -perfectly-sure-god-s-story-never.

15 http://www.encyclopedia.com/humanities/dictionaries -thesauruses-pictures-and-press-releases/discernment.

16 https://lenski.com/how-to-let-go-of-unresolved-conflict.

17 http://www.sermonsearch.com/sermon-illustrations/1084/not -today.

18 https://www.brainyquote.com/quotes/quotes/t/theodorero380703 .html.

19 https://www.goodreads.com/quotes/230436-over-the-years-i-have -come-to-realize-that-the.

20 Ibid.

21 https://www.brainyquote.com/quotes/quotes/g/georgewash158549 .html.

22 http://www.healanxietyanddepression.com.

23 https://www.brainyquote.com/quotes/quotes/a/abrahamlin383153 .html.

24 http://www.success.com/article/how-to-stand-up-for-yourself.

25 https://www.goodreads.com/quotes/51815-public-opinion-is-a
    -weak-tyrant-compared-with-our-own.

26 https://www.sciencedaily.com/releases/2011/08/110815162348
    .htm.

27 http://www.isacs.org/misc_files/SelfEsteem_Report%20-%20Dove
    %20Campaign%20for%20Real%20Beauty.pdf.

28 https://www.goodreads.com/quotes/63061-what-we-hope-ever-to
    -do-with-ease-we-must.

29 https://www.goodreads.com/quotes/42890-how-poor-are-they-that
    -have-not-patience-what-wound.

Do you have a real relationship with Jesus?

God loves you! He created you to be a special, unique, one-of-a-kind individual, and He has a specific purpose and plan for your life. And through a personal relationship with your Creator—God—you can discover a way of life that will truly satisfy your soul.

No matter who you are, what you've done, or where you are in your life right now, God's love and grace are greater than your sin—your mistakes. Jesus willingly gave His life so you can receive forgiveness from God and have new life in Him. He's just waiting for you to invite Him to be your Savior and Lord.

If you are ready to commit your life to Jesus and follow Him, all you have to do is ask Him to forgive your sins and give you a fresh start in the life you are meant to live. Begin by praying this prayer...

> *Lord Jesus, thank You for giving Your life for me and forgiving me of my sins so I can have a personal relationship with You. I am sincerely sorry for the mistakes I've made, and I know I need You to help me live right.*
>
> *Your Word says in Romans 10:9, "If you declare with your mouth, 'Jesus is Lord,' and believe in your heart that God raised him from the dead, you will be saved" (NIV). I believe You are the Son of God and confess You as my Savior and Lord. Take me just as I am, and work in my heart, making me the person You want me to be. I want to live for You, Jesus, and I am so grateful that You are giving me a fresh start in my new life with You today.*
>
> *I love You, Jesus!*

It's so amazing to know that God loves us so much! He wants to have a deep, intimate relationship with us that grows every day as we spend time with Him in prayer and Bible study. And we want to encourage you in your new life in Christ.

Please visit joycemeyer.org/salvation to request Joyce's book *A New Way of Living*, which is our gift to you. We also have other free resources online to help you make progress in pursuing everything God has for you.

Congratulations on your fresh start in your life in Christ! We hope to hear from you soon.

ABOUT THE AUTHOR

Joyce Meyer is one of the world's leading practical Bible teachers. A *New York Times* bestselling author, Joyce's books have helped millions of people find hope and restoration through Jesus Christ. Joyce's programs, *Enjoying Everyday Life* and *Everyday Answers with Joyce Meyer*, air around the world on television, radio, and the Internet. Through Joyce Meyer Ministries, Joyce teaches internationally on a number of topics with a particular focus on how the Word of God applies to our everyday lives. Her candid communication style allows her to share openly and practically about her experiences so others can apply what she has learned to their lives.

Joyce has authored more than one hundred books, which have been translated into more than one hundred languages, and over 65 million of her books have been distributed worldwide. Bestsellers include *Power Thoughts*; *The Confident Woman*; *Look Great, Feel Great*; *Starting Your Day Right*; *Ending Your Day Right*; *Approval Addiction*; *How to Hear from God*; *Beauty for Ashes*; and *Battlefield of the Mind*.

Joyce's passion to help hurting people is foundational to the vision of Hand of Hope, the missions arm of Joyce Meyer Ministries. Hand of Hope provides worldwide humanitarian outreaches such as feeding programs, medical care, orphanages, disaster response, human trafficking intervention and rehabilitation, and much more—always sharing the love and gospel of Christ.

JOYCE MEYER MINISTRIES
US AND FOREIGN OFFICE ADDRESSES

Joyce Meyer Ministries
P.O. Box 655
Fenton, MO 63026
USA
(636) 349-0303

Joyce Meyer Ministries—Canada
P.O. Box 7700
Vancouver, BC V6B 4E2
Canada
(800) 868-1002

Joyce Meyer Ministries—Australia
Locked Bag 77
Mansfield Delivery Centre
Queensland 4122
Australia
(07) 3349 1200

Joyce Meyer Ministries—England
P.O. Box 1549
Windsor SL4 1GT
United Kingdom
01753 831102

Joyce Meyer Ministries—South Africa
P.O. Box 5
Cape Town 8000
South Africa
(27) 21-701-1056

OTHER BOOKS BY JOYCE MEYER

100 Ways to Simplify Your Life
21 Ways to Finding Peace and Happiness
Any Minute
Approval Addiction
The Approval Fix
The Battle Belongs to the Lord
Battlefield of the Mind*
Battlefield of the Mind for Kids
Battlefield of the Mind for Teens
Battlefield of the Mind Devotional
Be Anxious for Nothing*
Being the Person God Made You to Be
Beauty for Ashes
Change Your Words, Change Your Life
The Confident Mom
The Confident Woman
The Confident Woman Devotional
Do Yourself a Favor…Forgive
Eat the Cookie…Buy the Shoes
Eight Ways to Keep the Devil under Your Feet
Ending Your Day Right
Enjoying Where You Are on the Way to Where You Are Going
The Everyday Life Bible
Filled with the Spirit
Good Health, Good Life
Hearing from God Each Morning
How to Hear from God*
How to Succeed at Being Yourself
I Dare You
If Not for the Grace of God*
In Pursuit of Peace
The Joy of Believing Prayer
Knowing God Intimately
A Leader in the Making
Life in the Word
Living Beyond Your Feelings
Living Courageously
Look Great, Feel Great
Love Out Loud
The Love Revolution
Making Good Habits, Breaking Bad Habits

Making Marriage Work (previously published as *Help Me—I'm Married!*)
*Me and My Big Mouth!**
*The Mind Connection**
Never Give Up!
Never Lose Heart
New Day, New You
Overload
The Penny
Perfect Love (previously published as *God Is Not Mad at You*)*
The Power of Being Positive
The Power of Being Thankful
The Power of Determination
The Power of Forgiveness
The Power of Simple Prayer
Power Thoughts
Power Thoughts Devotional
Reduce Me to Love
The Secret Power of Speaking God's Word
The Secrets of Spiritual Power
The Secret to True Happiness
Seven Things That Steal Your Joy
Start Your New Life Today
Starting Your Day Right
Straight Talk
Teenagers Are People Too!
Trusting God Day by Day
The Word, the Name, the Blood
Woman to Woman
You Can Begin Again

JOYCE MEYER SPANISH TITLES

Belleza en Lugar de Cenizas (*Beauty for Ashes*)
Buena Salud, Buena Vida (*Good Health, Good Life*)
Cambia Tus Palabras, Cambia Tu Vida (*Change Your Words, Change Your Life*)
El Campo de Batalla de la Mente (*Battlefield of the Mind*)
Como Formar Buenos Habitos y Romper Malos Habitos (*Making Good Habits, Breaking Bad Habits*)
La Conexión de la Mente (*The Mind Connection*)
Dios No Está Enojado Contigo (*God Is Not Mad at You*)
La Dosis de Aprobación (*The Approval Fix*)

Empezando Tu Día Bien (Starting Your Day Right)
Hazte un Favor a Ti Mismo...Perdona (Do Yourself a Favor...Forgive)
Madre Segura de sí Misma (The Confident Mom)
Pensamientos de Poder (Power Thoughts)
Sobrecarga (Overload)*
Termina Bien tu Día (Ending Your Day Right)
Usted Puede Comenzar de Nuevo (You Can Begin Again)
Viva Valientemente (Living Courageously)

* Study guide available for this title

BOOKS BY DAVE MEYER

Life Lines

Many women and girls all over the world are living in desperate situations, impacted by poverty, marginalized by society, or unaware of how very precious they truly are. Joyce's personal journey of healing and restoration has sparked in her a passion to help women and girls suffering with those same wounds and to help them become the masterpieces God created them to be.

This is the driving force behind **Project GRL**, an outreach of Joyce Meyer Ministries that empowers women and girls in all walks of life and cultures to discover their true identity in Christ. The mission of Project GRL is simply this: **Guide** them to fulfill their God-given potential, **Restore** their self-worth, and **Love** them to wholeness in Christ.

By providing clean water, nutritious meals, education, and safety from the horrors of human trafficking and other abusive environments, women and girls in many countries who feel hopeless are given the opportunity to know Christ and develop their true potential. And women everywhere will discover the amazing transformation of healing through Christ—spirit, soul and body, as the Gospel of Jesus Christ is the core message behind everything we do.

The needs are great, and you can help other women and girls experience the same healing and restoration in Christ that you have found. Visit **ProjectGRL.org** today.

Journaling is a profound tool for enhancing your spiritual journey, and it can allow you to get to the heart of what you see inside of yourself. There are no right or wrong answers here. Just be open and honest with yourself and with God, and you'll find what you are looking for.

*   *   *

Ephesians 1:17–18 says you have received the spirit of wisdom and revelation in the knowledge of Jesus, the eyes of your understanding being enlightened. After reading *Healing the Soul of a Woman*, do you understand yourself more? How will you continue your healing process from here? Journal your thoughts.

_____

_____

_____

_____

_____

_____

_____

_____

_____

_____

God supplies all of our needs according to His riches (Philippians 4:19), and what He has in mind for us is immeasurably better than what we give up. Is it difficult for you to let go of something you know you should give to God? If so, identify what it is and why.

_____

_____

_____

_____

_____

_____

_____

_____

_____

_____

_____

_____

_____

_____

1 Peter 2:9 says you show forth the praises of God, who has called you out of darkness into His marvelous light. Write down the struggles God has helped you through, and how you have been made a new creature in Christ.

_____

_____

_____

_____

_____

_____

_____

_____

_____

_____

_____

_____

_____

_____

_____

_____

Throughout the Bible, God says you are greatly loved (Romans 1:7; Ephesians 2:4–5; Colossians 3:12; 1 Thessalonians 1:4). Journal five declarations that will remind you that you are His beloved. Affirm yourself daily, and pray every morning that His truth will be shown to you.

_____

_____

_____

_____

_____

_____

_____

_____

_____

_____

_____

_____

_____

_____

Faith not only guides you in your daily walk; it protects you. When you truly believe that you have been made right with God through faith in Christ, you can overcome feeling guilty, condemned, and ashamed. Ephesians 6:16 says you can quench all the fiery darts of the wicked one with your shield of faith. What does this verse mean to you? How does it feel to know you are kept safe by God?

_____

_____

_____

_____

_____

_____

_____

_____

_____

_____

_____

_____

_____

You are God's workmanship, created in Christ unto good works (Ephesians 2:10). Celebrate who you are, and write down at least five things you love about yourself. Say a prayer of thanks that you were created in His image.

_____

_____

_____

_____

_____

_____

_____

_____

_____

_____

_____

_____

_____

_____

James 1:22–25 says that if you do what God shows you to do in His Word, you will be blessed in your actions. Journal about how you can live out this concept. What can you do throughout your day to "do the Word"?

_____

_____

_____

_____

_____

_____

_____

_____

_____

_____

_____

_____

_____

_____

_____

_____

Romans 8:17 says you are a joint-heir with Christ. Write this verse in your own words, and meditate on the fact that your inheritance in God is greater than any trouble you may endure.

_____

_____

_____

_____

_____

_____

_____

_____

_____

_____

_____

_____

_____

What do you think it means to be more than a conqueror in Christ (Romans 8:37)? Do you believe this about yourself? Journal about why or why not, and write a prayer asking God to increase your faith so you can see yourself as a conqueror.

_____

_____

_____

_____

_____

_____

_____

_____

_____

_____

_____

_____

_____

_____

We are called to be firmly rooted in Christ, built up, established in faith, and overflowing with gratitude in Colossians 2:7. Write down the scriptures that root you, and journal about at least three things for which you are grateful in your healing journey.

_____

_____

_____

_____

_____

_____

_____

_____

_____

_____

_____

_____

_____

_____

_____

_____

Revelation 12:11 says you are an overcomer by the blood of the Lamb and the word of your testimony. Have you shared your testimony with anyone since reading *Healing the Soul of a Woman*? Has it changed at all? Write about it here, and focus on your progress instead of how far you have to go.

_____

_____

_____

_____

_____

_____

_____

_____

_____

_____

_____

_____

_____

_____

You are strengthened with all might according to His glorious power (Colossians 1:11). Who in your life also strengthens and supports you? Write about how they lift you up and assist you in your healing journey. Say a prayer of thanks to God for bringing them into your life.

_____

_____

_____

_____

_____

_____

_____

_____

_____

_____

_____

_____

_____

_____

Deuteronomy 28:13 says you are the head and not the tail; you are above only and not beneath. Write about five things you are *not*. What do these things say about you and your journey to healing?

_____

_____

_____

_____

_____

_____

_____

_____

_____

_____

_____

_____

_____

_____

_____

_____

We as believers are part of a chosen generation, a holy nation (1 Peter 2:9). How can you uplift other women who may be struggling? How will you use your story to share the love of Christ?

_____

_____

_____

_____

_____

_____

_____

_____

_____

_____

_____

_____

_____

_____

What are your hopes and desires for the future, as Jesus mends your pain and suffering? What do you long for? Ask God to guide you and give Him the glory for future blessings.

_____

_____

_____

_____

_____

_____

_____

_____

_____

_____

_____

_____

_____

_____

_____

_____

_____

Isaiah 53:5 says we are healed by the stripes of Jesus, and we are called of God to be the voice of His praise (Psalm 66:8). Write a prayer of gratitude to God for saving you and healing your soul.

_____

_____

_____

_____

_____

_____

_____

_____

_____

_____

_____

_____

_____

_____

_____

_____